THE
REBIRTH
OF
MINISTRY

*A Study of the Biblical Character
of the Church's Ministry*

THE

REBIRTH

OF

MINISTRY

by James D. Smart

The Westminster Press
Philadelphia

Library of Congress Catalog Card No. 60–6189

9 8 7 6 5 4 3 2 1

PRINTED IN THE UNITED STATES OF AMERICA

CONTENTS

67658

FOREWORD
TO THE PAPERBACK EDITION

In this foreword to the paperback edition of THE REBIRTH OF MINISTRY, I am glad to reaffirm its overall representation of the ministry, and I am not able to see any reason for a basic revision. The reader should be reminded, however, that this is a reprinting of what was written eighteen years ago and that I am aware of the need today for some things to be stated differently. For instance, the Second Vatican Council and the widespread influence of a fresh approach to Scripture in the Catholic Church make pages 175-176 quite out of date. Also the depreciation of Judaism on pages 43-44 is now an embarrassment to me. Judaism and Christianity have too much in common for us to do more than spell out as sympathetically as possible the points of agreement and divergence between them. A Jewish rabbi in intimate fellowship with the prophets of Israel may be closer to the ministry of Jesus than a Christian minister whose Jesus has been completely divorced from the prophetic tradition and made into a modern purveyor of sweetness and light.

I wrote this book when I was fresh out of years of wrestling with problems of ministry in several different parishes and was being forced to evaluate my experiences by the questions of seminary students. Having been in the pastorate again from 1970 to 1974, I benefited from the clarification which the writing of the book had brought me. To some readers the optimism and self-confidence of Christians in the late 1950's, which is criticized here, will seem very remote. What is remarkable is that so much of this self-satisfaction remains in our North American churches. There are ministers and people who are unshaken by the events of the last two decades and still think of their churches as reasonably Christian societies in a Christian nation. The Vietnam war, the civil rights struggle, the assassinations, the Watergate trials, the "death of God" theology, the oil embargo wakening us to a sudden awareness of the fragility of the structures of our society, the uncontrollable arms budget swallowing up a nation's resources, the widening gap between rich and poor nations, the pollution of the environment — all combine, however, to shake us out of any complacency that we have left. And in this time of shaking and being shaken perhaps there may be a greater willingness to consider what a really Christian ministry can mean to our world.

The problem discussed in Chapter 3, "The Ministry of the Word," I have investigated in much greater detail in *The Strange Silence of the Bible in the Church,* published in 1970. The ever-present problem, that without our realizing it our Biblical faith may be so elided with our cultural allegiances that it loses its cutting edge, I have discussed recently in *The Cultural Subversion of the Biblical Faith.*

As before, this book is dedicated to James Dutton and Abbie Ada Dutton, for whom the call to the Christian life was a call to ministry.

JAMES D. SMART

PREFACE

THIS book had its origin very gradually during twenty years in the pastorate as the conviction grew steadily that in all our churches both the ministry and the Christian congregation have lost much of their essential Biblical character. I dealt extensively with one aspect of the problem in *The Teaching Ministry of the Church* (The Westminster Press, 1954), but I was acutely aware that the subject needed much broader exploration. In March, 1958, in the Gay Lectures at Southern Baptist Seminary in Louisville, Kentucky, I had opportunity to develop four themes in a preliminary fashion in lectures that have now been expanded in Chapters 1, 2, 3, and 8. Chapter 2 was published in the magazine of the Southern Baptist Seminary, the *Review and Expositor,* in July, 1958. Then in February, 1959, the Weber Memorial Lectures, delivered at the Moravian Theological Seminary in Bethlehem, Pennsylvania, contained material that has been refashioned and further developed in Chapters 5 and 6.

I am fully aware that I have left many problems regarding the ministry untouched. A chapter might have been devoted to a review of the discussions of the ministry in the Faith and Order Conferences of the ecumenical movement. It is at this point that different churches seem to have had the greatest difficulty in reaching a basis for mutual recognition and that the ecumenical discussions have seemed to reach a sterile stalemate. Each church is so certain that in its own order it is safeguarding and preserving the essential ministry of the church without which the church itself would be lost. But perhaps there would be more progress if there were more thorough investigation by all the churches of what the essential ministry is at its point of origin as witnessed to by the Scriptures. Then, as each church considered its own present ministry in the light of the ministry of prophets and apostles, with Jesus Christ at their center, it would be forced to confess that all our churches are failing to embody the fullness of *that* ministry. The Biblical ministry would thus become the point of reorientation so that, instead of attempting to find some form of compromise between our existing orders of ministry in order to achieve unity, a more vital process of reformation would be set in motion and the churches would realize a profounder unity with one another as they found themselves coming together in a more truly prophetic and apostolic ministry. It is to be hoped that from this angle the present book may make some contribution, however small, to ecumenical understanding. It may seem to stand strongly in the Reformed tradition, but perhaps at some points it will be seen that the author has been influenced by the contributions of other traditions.

Problems of ministry in the younger churches have not been considered specifically, but they have been kept in mind. Many of these churches, because of their merging of a variety of ecclesiastical traditions in one church, are being forced to make decisions quickly on matters that the older churches discuss leisurely over a long period of years. Surely, if these churches are not only to profit by the experience of the older churches but also to avoid our costly errors, the only sound procedure for them is to study their own particular problems of ministry in the light of what the ministry is in the Scriptures, with the centuries of trial and error in all the churches as a commentary and guide, and, above all, to ask what form of ministry the gospel demands of them in their situation today.

The conception of ministry as it is developed in these pages has implications for theological education, but this does not seem to be the proper place to deal with them, since the book is addressed in general to all who profess the Christian faith, and in particular to those who are active in some phase of the parish ministry or in preparation for it. If the concept of the "wholeness" of the ministry is valid, then the various departments of the theological curriculum should be much more closely integrated than they are. The student should not be left to find the hidden unity, if he can, in the fragmented studies that are presented to him by departments that often have not even discussed with one another the interrelation of their respective disciplines. Also there needs to be thorough consideration of what effect it would have upon each of the theological disciplines if it were approached as a ministry *of* the church, *in* the church, and *for* the church, rather than as a discipline that is primarily academic and only in some secondary fashion related to the life of the church.

Perhaps to some it will seem a very great weakness in this presentation that it nowhere establishes a clear line of distinction between the ministry of an ordained clergy and the ministry of the whole church. Does ordination mean nothing more than that the person ordained is a special instance of a ministry that in principle belongs to all believers? Are there not powers, privileges, and responsibilities conferred by ordination that belong only to those who are ordained? That there is need of a special ministry, called of God and set apart for a special service of God within his church, stands forth clearly in Scripture. All Israel was chosen of God to be a nation of prophets and priests in the midst of mankind, but that vision of destiny was kept alive only by a succession of special prophets and priests. All who responded in faith to Jesus Christ were called to minister and bear witness among their fellow men, but the Twelve, and others later, were chosen for a special ministry without which the church would not have long endured. But nowhere in Scripture can there be found a clear line of distinction between the ministry that belongs to the whole Israel of God and the ministry that belongs to those who are specially set apart. Moreover, when such a line is drawn sharply and deeply, the consequence is that the essential ministry of Jesus Christ is consigned exclusively to an ordained clergy and ceases to be considered as belonging in any way to the ordinary believer. The thesis of this book is that baptism and confirmation are the primary ordination to the ministry of Jesus Christ to which all else is secondary; in short, that according to the Scriptures, one cannot be a Christian without receiving the Spirit of God, which is always empowerment for a ministry. Only when this primary ordination has its true meaning restored to it do special ordinations find their proper context. We need a high view of the office of the ordained minister and elder, but even more we need a high view of the office of the Christian believer and disciple, and it would be very strange if the latter should in any way detract from the former, as some churchmen seem to fear. Surely the more truly the whole Israel of God knows and claims its ministry, the more will special ministries within the Israel of God be held in honor and fulfill their destined function.

New York   J.D.S.

1

AN APOSTOLIC MINISTRY

ONE of the primary distinguishing marks of a church that is faithful to its origins in the Scriptures and in the Reformation is its capacity for self-criticsm. It is able to say far more disturbing things about itself from within than any enemy is able to direct against it from without. Because it lives in utter dependence upon the judging, redeeming word of God, it is constantly humbled and shaken within itself by God's ruthless, searing critique of all things in its life.

We catch that note of self-criticism already in the New Testament in the portraits of themselves that the apostles left behind. They did not represent themselves as the great early heroes of the faith, spotless in virtue and unshaken in courage; rather, they confessed how blind they were, how slow to grasp the truth that confronted them in Jesus Christ, how ready to give way to human prejudices that alienated them from the spirit of Jesus. In the New Testament we do not have a perfect church and a perfect ministry taking over where Jesus left off. Far from it! Rather, we have men like ourselves, stumbling and sinful and able to get terribly confused, yet called into the ministry of Jesus Christ, commissioned with his gospel, and encouraged with the promise that, if they held fast to their faith in him, his Spirit would lead them into all truth. Their constant confession was that they were not yet what their Lord would have them be. The complete fulfillment of their apostolic ministry lay always before them as a promise. We think of Paul, far on in his amazingly fruitful ministry, confessing that he did not count himself to have as yet laid hold on the full meaning of his high calling, and expressing passionately the hope that he might be changed from likeness to likeness until he would be made like Jesus Christ in his ministry. (Phil. 3:14; II Cor. 3:18.)

THE CONFUSION OF OUR SITUATION

Self-criticism lies at the very heart of a Biblical and Protestant ministry. It is, therefore, not a reason for satisfaction that our American Protestantism at present is strong on confidence and weak in self-criticism. The statistics, which place over 60 per cent of the population on church rolls, seem to many to give a solid basis for confidence. So also do the huge but successful budgets of our churches and the crowded houses of worship. We find it very easy in our minds to say of ourselves, "We are a successful Christian church," and the corollary of that, of course, is, "We are successful Christian ministers." It would in many quarters be regarded as disloyalty to one's congregation, or one's denomination, to suggest that it is failing in any essential way. And it would certainly cause some consternation to suggest that our ministry, in spite of its outward success, is not what it was intended by our Lord to be and therefore in his sight a failure. And yet that is what needs desperately to be said. We are involved today on this continent in a colossal perversion of the church from its true nature and calling. It has its closest parallel in what happened to the church over sixteen hundred years ago in the days of Constantine. In the fourth century the church was adopted by Roman society. Millions of Romans flooded into it to swell its membership. But they brought with them their pagan culture and many elements of their pagan faith. They made the church a successful Roman church, full to overflowing, but it took the church more than one thousand years to recover from that success and to rediscover its true nature and calling. Something similar to that has been happening to us. In the twentieth century the church has been adopted by our American society. Millions of citizens have flooded into it to swell its membership. In most communities a person has to have his name on the membership roll of some church or synagogue in order to have any social standing. Will Herberg has documented this situation very convincingly in his sociological study of religion in America, *Protestant-Catholic-Jew*. His assertion is that church and synagogue alike have been infiltrated by a religion that is based on the values of our American civilization, and that has only the slightest continuity with traditional Protestantism, Roman Catholicism, or Judaism.

Herberg has put his finger on an acute sickness of the church that we ignore at our peril. But the diagnosis needs to be carried one stage farther. Even where the church has resisted the pressure to identify itself with our civilization, it has tended to become an institution for religious, moral, and social purposes that looks to Jesus Christ as its founder but has ceased to understand itself in New Testament terms as a body to be actually indwelt by him and so fashioned into an instrument for the continuation of his full redemptive work in the present day. The simple fact that confronts us is that the ordinary Christian no longer thinks of himself as committed in any personal way to live and work in that kind of closeness to Jesus Christ. The church is for him a religious institution to which he belongs and which he supports, and not a fellowship of disciples living in immediate communion with their Master and with his mission as the primary concern of their existence. He thinks of God and the church as existing for his sake, and it would be puzzling to him to hear that it is the other way around, that he is meant to have his existence for the sake of God and the church of God. This is the reality of the empirical church against which we beat our heads as against an iron wall and which makes a mockery again and again of the preaching of a gospel that calls men to discipleship, and of the sacrament of our Lord's body and blood in which we affirm our oneness with him. And this institution for religious, moral, and social purposes sucks our ministry into itself and makes us, perhaps unconsciously, *its* ministers rather than ministers of Jesus Christ. This is the primary perversion of the church and ministry that then makes possible the identification of the purposes of the church with the purposes of our civilization.

What makes this situation most dangerous is the lack in our American Protestantism of a critical theology that addresses itself directly to the problems of the church. The atmosphere of both church and society is not congenial to critical thinking. In general, affirmations are preferred to anything savoring of negation. Positive thinking in religion sells a million copies, but a seriously critical work in theology is not likely to secure a wide circulation. Also, much of the most serious writing concerning the Christian faith has in it the quality of the monologue rather than of the dialogue. It contents itself with the development of a theological or religious standpoint without any thoroughgoing critique of the various standpoints that are actually determining the life of the church. The most sharply critical thinking of recent years has been in the field of ethics and has concerned itself with the relation of Christianity to the problems of society and civilization. In systematic theology the concern has been more with the problems of Christianity and culture and the relation of theology to philosophy than with the theological issues that are implicit in the life and ministry of the church. The quality of monologue and the avoidance of theological controversy has made our American theological scene much less stimulating than it might be and has often served to obscure the importance of questions in the life of the church in which our very existence is involved. There can be no question but that our American Christianity, in spite of its impressive outward success, conceals within it weaknesses, confusions, and misunderstandings that must be brought into the open and overcome if they are not to endanger the future of the church, and of more than the church. The two questions that most immediately concern us are simply stated but not so simply answered: Are we the church of Jesus Christ that we claim to be? Are we the ministry of Jesus Christ that we claim to be?

We shall call two witnesses at this point, one American and one English, to support the contention that there exists a serious confusion about the purpose of the church and its ministry. In 1947, an English Congregational minister, Daniel T. Jenkins, published a study entitled *The Gift of Ministry*. He sees the problem of the ministry as significant not only for the church but also for the whole of modern society. For him the prevalent vagueness and uncertainty about the nature of the ministry is an intensified form of modern man's vagueness and uncertainty about his nature and function as a human being. Ceasing to understand rightly what man is here for and who he is, we have inevitably gone astray in our understanding of what is involved in our ministry to men. The minister in England, says Dr. Jenkins, is not quite sure how he is meant to function as a minister and unfortunately finds himself most acceptable in society when he least resembles the New Testament type of ministry. And because the minister is unsure of himself, the average Englishman, though generally well disposed toward him, does not understand him or know what to expect of him.

But we have evidence from closer at hand in the books published under the direction of H. Richard Niebuhr and Daniel Day Williams in their restudy of the ministry in relation to theological education: H. Richard Niebuhr, *The Purpose of the Church and Its Ministry* (Harper & Brothers, 1956); H. Richard Niebuhr and Daniel Day Williams, *The Ministry in Historical Perspectives* (Harper & Brothers, 1956); H. Richard Niebuhr, Daniel Day Williams, James M. Gustafson, *The Advancement of Theological Education* (Harper & Brothers, 1957). From their sifting of evidence from ministers and laymen and from our theological seminaries, they assert unequivocally that at the heart of the problem is an inability of our churches to say what a minister is intended to be. There is no scarcity of persons who are quite confident that they can answer that question, but when the answers are on paper, they merely add new evidence that the church is in deep confusion about its ministry. What is a minister? He is an evangelist. He is a preacher. He is a priest. He is a religious administrator. He is a social reformer. He is a director of worth-while enterprises for the community. He is a species of amateur psychiatrist. He is an educator. He is an interpreter of life somewhat in the fashion of the poet. He is the voice of the community's conscience. He is the custodian of the values of democratic civilization. He is a man of superior wisdom and virtue whose task each week is to show men and women how to live more wisely and virtuously. Is it any wonder that young ministers, and some not so young, find themselves dragged in a dozen different directions as they try to fulfill the claims of the ministry? Dr. Niebuhr points out that in the medieval church there was a clear-cut picture of the minister as the director of souls, in the Reformation church an equally clear-cut picture of the minister as the preacher of the word, and in Pietism the minister as evangelist, but that in twentieth-century Protestantism no such unitary and unifying principle exists.

The two criticisms that may most validly be raised in regard to Dr. Niebuhr's presentation are, first, that he does not relate the church's confusion about the nature of its ministry to the deeper problem of the church's confusion about its own nature and function (which also involves a ministry of a very definite kind), and, secondly, that he does not point with any decisiveness to the formulation of the ministry in the Scriptures as the source of a valid criterion that might enable us to find the way out of our confusion. In both these respects Jenkins speaks much more convincingly and helpfully, recognizing as he does that there is no hope for us until we redefine both church and ministry in the light of their origin in Jesus Christ.

The Criterion of Our Ministry

The essential nature of the Christian ministry has been determined for all time by the ministry of Jesus Christ. All our thinking must take his person and ministry as its starting point. That does not mean that the form of our ministry is to be copied directly from the Gospels and must remain the same in all ages. All things in the life of the church — its doctrine, its ritual, its organizational patterns, its cultural formulations — must be redefined from time to time, partly because they share the corruption of all things human and are in need of further transformation and partly because the world that is to be redeemed refuses to stay the same. The mortality rate for old sermons is higher than for any other human production for these same two reasons. The preacher, if there is any work of redemption going forward in his own life, is a different man, a wiser man; and the people to whom he speaks are no longer the same people that they were a year before. The church must have in it an infinite capacity for mobility and adaptability and dare not freeze into static and immovable forms. And yet the test of its integrity remains the same — whether or not it is the church after the mind of Christ and the true continuation of the apostolic church as we see it in the New Testament. The same is true of the church's ministry. It must in the fullest sense be a ministry to our age; it must speak a language that men of our age can understand; and yet at the same time it must be the ministry of Jesus Christ in the twentieth century based firmly on what we know of the ministry of Jesus Christ in the first century. The clarification of these two concerns will engage our attention constantly throughout this study.

This fundamental assertion of principle goes directly contrary to a widespread and popular idea, the idea that we are free as Christian ministers to make of the ministry whatever we will in the light of the needs of our day. This is often the consequence of an interpretation of the New Testament that alleges that Jesus merely preached his gospel and left the form of the ministry as a secondary matter to be determined by the church in each new age as might seem expedient. We receive the gospel from him but not the form of our ministry. Where this interpretation prevails, the fact is concealed that in both the life of Jesus and the lives of his apostles the nature of the gospel demanded that the ministry should be shaped in certain definite directions. One instance will be sufficient at this point: it is a gospel of God's love for men that compels Jesus to go in search of the lost sheep of the house of Israel. That form of ministry is therefore as obligatory as the gospel itself. We are not free to have a ministry that is not concerned about lost sheep. But, having declared our freedom in regard to forms, we are no longer bound by the form of Jesus' ministry. The consequence is that unrestrained individualism has long been the order of the day in most of our Protestant churches, determining not only the shape of the ministry but many other things as well. The insistence, therefore, that there is an essential structure both to the ministry and to the whole life of the Christian church that we abandon at peril of reverting into chaos is likely to be regarded as an unwarranted interference with the liberty of the individual minister and the individual church.

It is at this point that contemporary thinking about the ministry must be decisively challenged. The ministry into which we enter is the ministry *of Jesus Christ*. We are not free to determine its nature as we will; its nature has already been determined for us by his life, death, and resurrection and by the work of his Spirit in the shaping of the apostolic ministry. That is, in part, the significance of the line that the second-century church drew around the canonical books of Scripture. These were the books in which it found the nature of its gospel, the nature of the church, and the nature of the church's ministry defined once and for all. Therefore, if we want to know what our ministry is, we must go to the Scriptures and trace out the line that runs from the Old Testament ministry through the ministry of Jesus and directly forward through the ministry of the apostles and so across the centuries to us. The supreme test of any ministry that claims to be Christian is whether or not it is a valid continuation of that line. It is not sufficient, as some churches hold, that there should be an unbroken line of human transmission by laying on of hands from the apostles to the present day. Apostolic succession is witness to something very important in so far as it reminds us that we are no true church unless we stand in direct succession to the church of the apostles. Our faith is a true faith only as it is one with theirs. Our ministry is a true ministry only as it is a faithful continuation of their ministry in the modern world. But the communication of faith and ministry from them to us, though it is historically a process of nineteen centuries, is not endangered by weak links in the chain of succession so long as the apostles themselves through the medium of Scripture can speak directly to each new generation. That which is indispensable is the communication by them of that which they received as a trust for all mankind, the communication through Word and Spirit of the very mind and heart and redemptive power that reside in our Lord himself.

The Form of Jesus' Ministry

It is crucial, then, for us to grasp with the utmost clarity the character of Jesus' ministry. But the question of his ministry cannot be separated from two prior questions concerning his gospel and his person. What Jesus said, what he was, and what he did are all aspects of a single reality. Therefore, his ministry cannot be described in isolation. Nor can his teaching. His person is the concealed center of all his teaching and preaching. His ministry is the concrete expression of his person. This can be illustrated from the Sermon on the Mount and the parables, which are sometimes regarded as containing an ethic that is independent of Jesus' person.

The Sermon on the Mount has its true meaning only in the context of the intimate relation between Jesus and disciples who, in response to him, have accepted not only poverty but also the intolerable strains of an exacting ministry and the likelihood of hostility from their fellow countrymen. They are the poor, who have had their eyes opened by Jesus to see the poverty of their present condition before God. They are the mourners, who have learned from Jesus that to be really open toward God is to be open also toward the sufferings, sorrows, and anxieties of their fellow men. They are the meek, who have been utterly humbled by the claim that a sovereign God makes upon them. They are the merciful, who have learned a new approach to the whole problem of human sin through Jesus' dealing with *their* sin. The Sermon on the Mount was not intended to be a practicable ethic for the human race in general. Rather, it is a description of the new life opened to men by Jesus Christ alone and practicable only for men who through him have had their sins forgiven and have begun to live their lives by the immediate grace and power of God's indwelling Spirit.

Also, in the parables the gospel of Jesus and the person of Jesus are inseparable. When any one of them is extracted from its original situation in which Jesus was addressing some particular person or persons, a meaning is read off the surface that is little more than a superficial moral, readily available in many other quarters. "Be kind to anyone in need." "Be sure to use your talents." But when the parable is read in the context in which it first occurred (where that is possible), it is evident at once that it was not spoken to point an easy moral or to illustrate a spiritual truth but was an instrument used by Jesus to discover men to themselves. He hid the person or persons whom he was addressing in what seemed a simple story, but in such a way that they unwittingly passed judgment upon themselves. The truth of the man's condition in relation to God was hidden in the story, so that to understand the story was to see how one stood with God. (Luke 7:41 f.; 10:25 ff.; 15:1 ff.; 18:9 ff.) But if the addressee was hidden in the parable, so also was Jesus himself. It is through him that the good news is given to debtors that their debts are forgiven freely. (Luke 7:41 f.) He himself is the despised Samaritan who cannot go past the broken man at the roadside. (Luke 10:25 ff.) It is in him that the father goes down the road to meet the son who is returning. (Luke, ch. 15.) It is where he stands that the line becomes visible between the charitable, scrupulously pious man whose trust is ultimately in his own religiousness and the renegade with little to recommend him outwardly but whose trust is wholly in the mercy of God. (Luke 18:9 ff.) Can there be any doubt that the man who found himself in any one of Jesus' parables would find not only himself but also the One who was able to discover him to himself because of his uncanny power of knowing men as only God knows them? The mystery of Jesus' person is at the very center of his parables.

But if Jesus' gospel and his person are inseparable, it is equally true that his person and his ministry are inseparable, for what do we know of his person except in his ministry? The four Gospels concentrate their attention exclusively upon his ministry. They have no interest in biographical details of the kind that we are accustomed to call "personal." This has led some scholars to the extreme and mistaken conclusion that we know nothing of Jesus' person but only his gospel. The life of Jesus apart from his ministry, the thirty years in his home in Nazareth, the incidentals of his life with his disciples that would be so significant in portraying his personality, are almost entirely hidden from us. But the life of Jesus in which he fulfilled his ministry as One sent from God to preach the gospel to the poor, to heal the broken-hearted, to set the prisoners free, is not hidden from us. Rather, it is very fully documented, and it is in that ministry that we know him as the person that he was. His ministry is unique, even as his gospel and his person are unique, and all three must be understood together.

It offended Jesus' contemporaries that they could fit his ministry into none of the categories that were familiar to them. He was neither priest nor rabbi. When they tried to classify him as a prophet with John the Baptist, he accused them of the folly of putting his new wine in old wineskins and claimed freedom to fulfill his ministry in untraditional ways. His gospel had to be free to shape his ministry according to its own intrinsic pattern. But what is that pattern?

We have already drawn attention to the itinerant character of Jesus' ministry as he sought everywhere for his lost sheep. In this it is contrasted sharply with that of John the Baptist. Men in search of God sought out John. God in search of man sent Jesus into the towns and villages of Palestine to find his lost sons. With Jesus began the invasion of the life of our humanity by God, and the first stage of that invasion, what we might call the beach-head of that invasion, was God's total possession of the existence of Jesus himself. The ministry of Jesus was therefore rooted and grounded in the joy of his own fulfillment in God. It was the oneness of his own humanity with God that gave his ministry from the beginning the character of a ministry of reconciliation.

A second obvious characteristic is Jesus' proclamation of the Kingdom. He was a herald of God. The term "gospel" for his preaching and teaching he found in Second Isaiah, where it is used to describe the good news of what God is about to do for his despairing people. (Cf. Isa. 40:9; 52:7; etc.) The exclusion of Jesus' teaching from the "gospel" or "kerygma," which has become customary since it was first suggested by C. H. Dodd, has no basis in the Gospels themselves and leads to a quite false conception of his teaching. The good news is that God has not forgotten his promise. What he is doing may be hidden for the moment but only for the moment. Because God is God, Creator of the worlds and Lord of history, his sovereign purpose must prevail, and his people can live in confidence that his Kingdom of justice and truth will be established. But was Jesus, then, herald only of a Kingdom yet to come? One school of interpretation stemming from Schweitzer insists that for Jesus the Kingdom was wholly future, and there are many texts in the Gospels that seem to support their view. Another school of interpretation, of which C. H. Dodd is the chief representative, holds to a theory of realized eschatology, insisting, with considerable justice, that many passages in the Gospels make no sense unless the Kingdom was already present. The antithesis between the two rests upon a misunderstanding of Biblical eschatology. For Second Isaiah or for Jesus or for Paul to say "God is coming" is actually a way of saying "God is sovereign." It is faith in God's sovereignty over his world that gives birth to eschatology. The believer lives through the hours of darkness without despairing because he believes that God was, is, and shall be sovereign. His rule may be hidden in the present moment, but it can be seen by looking to the past and it will be vindicated in the future. Jesus' proclamation of God's rule (i.e., Kingdom) has therefore to do with both present and future. To come under God's present personal rule is to receive him in his sovereign Spirit to indwell one's being. Since man in his self-sovereignty resists God's rule, the self must be broken out of the center, must be humbled, must be denied, must die, if God is to be sovereign. But so to die is to come alive to God, or to be reborn and to live in the world as a new person. Not wholly new, for the self never wholly dies but lives on to resist God to the very end, so that man is never done repenting or praying for God's Kingdom to come and God's Spirit to be given. The Kingdom that is proclaimed is by its nature both present and future, for it is nothing other than God's sovereignty.

But how could Jesus proclaim the Kingdom with such confidence? Again the secret lies in his own person. He proclaims the Kingdom not as something beyond himself but always as a reality that he knows from within. He lived in the presence and power of the Kingdom because he lived as the One in whom God's Spirit ruled absolutely. Where he stands God *is* sovereign. His perfect obedience to the will of God is therefore one of the surest signs of the presence of the Kingdom in him. So also is the perfectness of God's love and God's truth and God's purity in him. To Jesus himself his works of healing and exorcism were signs of God's present rule, and he equated the presence of the Spirit with the presence of the Kingdom. " If it is by the Spirit of God that I cast out demons, then the kingdom of God has come upon you." (Matt. 12:28.) Again it must be said that hidden in his proclamation of the Kingdom is a claim, unspoken, concerning his own person. Only at the last, when there was no longer any possibility of misunderstanding, could he let it be said openly that he was the King.

A third characteristic, more central to Jesus' ministry than is sometimes realized, was his forgiveness of men's sins. His purpose was the restoration of men to their true life in God. Man, cut apart from God, was a poor, broken, unhappy creature. The consequences of his alienation from God were not just spiritual, but also physical and social. A man lives in his relationships, not first in himself and then in his relations with others; and what he is in his relation with God cannot be kept separate from what he is in his relation with men. The two are in constant interaction. How could it be otherwise, then, but that sin, in which a man finds a barrier thrust up between himself and God, should bring confusion in all of life's relationships? The presence of sin and all its ruinous consequences in human life stirred in Jesus not anger but compassion; it was the denial of sin by any man that stirred his scorn. To him all men were sick with the poison of sin, and his mission was that of a physician who could save them from sickness and death. His remedy was God's infinite forgiveness, not any cheap condoning of sin and letting men off from punishment, but rather a holy love in which judgment and mercy were one, so that the sinner, by God's acceptance of him, was given the courage to face the full reality of his sin and yet in the same moment was made to loathe the sin that shut him out from God and to turn from it with all his heart. Forgiveness as it was known in Jesus Christ was God's better way of dealing with sin, so that it was literally torn up by the roots and not just restrained by fear of punishment. The forgiveness could not be separated from the Forgiver any more than God's Word can be separated from God. Therefore, to be forgiven by God was to receive the forgiving God, the God of infinite love himself, and the forgiven man became one in whom other men were met by the same infinite forgiveness that he himself had met in God. Forgiveness was thus one form of God's invasion of the world and his chief instrument in the conquest of evil, so that the ministry of Jesus was of necessity a ministry of forgiveness. Moreover, his claim, " The Son of man hath power on earth to forgive sins," was again a hidden way of asserting the claim of his unique Person.

A fourth characteristic of Jesus' ministry was his insistence that it must take the form of a servant. There are wide differences among scholars whether it was the early church or Jesus himself who introduced the servant figure of Second Isaiah into the interpretation of his ministry. Certainly from the earliest days of the church not only Philip (Acts 8:35) but Christians in general saw the death and resurrection of Jesus portrayed in Isa., ch. 53. The story of the cross represents Jesus in his last hours repeating the words of Ps. 22, which is in many ways a close parallel to Isa., ch. 53. There are many points of contact between the teaching of Second Isaiah and the teachings of Jesus, parallels that seem to show his familiarity with this part of the Old Testament. Jesus' mind and spirit being such as they were, it is impossible to think of his not being drawn to the great evangelist of the sixth century, the last great prophet before John the Baptist. It seems singularly unimaginative, therefore, to suppose that Jesus, in the conflicts and perils of his ministry, would pay no heed to what was written more than five centuries earlier concerning the bitter trials that could be expected by anyone who responded to God's call for a servant to be the bearer of his judging, saving word to Israel. As with the servant, in Isa., ch. 53, so also with Jesus it was hidden from the eyes of men that in him God's mighty arm was being revealed. He was despised and rejected. But only thus, only where there was a servant so completely faithful to God that he was willing to be despised and rejected, could God break through the stubborn resistance of men in their blindness and win his victory. Jesus not only claimed the servant-destiny for himself but did all in his power to make clear to his disciples that there would be no victories for them in the future unless they held fast to the form of a servant. Luke depicts Jesus beginning his ministry in the synagogue at Nazareth by interpreting his own mission as the fulfillment of the servant's mission heralded by Second Isaiah in Isa. 61:1-3. John depicts him on the last night of his life performing the office of the most menial servant of the household and washing the disciples' feet. The servant motif is deeply embedded in the tradition. To no Jew would it represent a claim of Messiahship, but rather the opposite, so that it too was a form of concealment for the true dimensions of Jesus' person.

Many New Testament scholars insist that Jesus had no consciousness of a Messianic ministry. They base their insistence upon the indisputable fact that there is no passage in the Synoptic Gospels in which Jesus clearly announces himself as the Messiah. But that fact may mean no more than that Jesus practiced a deliberate concealment of his Messiahship for the rather obvious reason that any claim of Messiahship would have been certain to create misunderstanding and that in its true meaning the knowledge of it could not be directly conveyed to anyone else. In his temptations Jesus is represented as repudiating the popular conceptions of the Messiah. But even among his disciples these popular conceptions persisted and the term " messiah " would not have meant to them what it did to Jesus. It took the cross to redeem the word "messiah" so that it could be used freely by the disciples concerning him. But this need not mean that Jesus repudiated it within himself, or that any evidence of a consciousness of Messiahship, as in the stories of the baptism and the temptations, must be attributed to the church's interpretation of Jesus. Rather, as we have seen, there seems to be conclusive evidence in his teachings, in his parables, and in his dealings with individuals, that he was constantly but in a concealed manner asserting a claim for his own person that is the expression either of a colossal egotism or of a consciousness of occupying an absolutely unique place and fulfilling an absolutely unique destiny in God's redemptive purpose for humanity.

All aspects of Jesus' ministry come to their climactic expression in the cross. Strangely, it was in his dying that his ministry was fulfilled with the profoundest power. Again we meet the oneness of gospel, ministry, and person. The cross, with which men thought to silence him once and for all, became the unveiling of the mystery of who he was and the instrument whereby he completed his ministry of reconciliation. The nails that fastened him to the cross set him free to invade the whole world, for it is in his dying that he breaks open the doors behind which men hide from him. The seeming victory of the world over the Kingdom at the cross was a hollow victory, for it is in his dying that Jesus stands forth as the only man among men who by what he is as God's man establishes his right to be Lord and Sovereign over all men. Not without reason the cross has also been the place where men have most readily found forgiveness, for there they see most easily the horror of their sin in what it does and the infinity of the love of God in Jesus Christ who would even die that they might be forgiven. Most clearly of all, as Second Isaiah well knew, the road of the servant, who could not compromise his knowledge of God in order to ease the tension between his fellow men and God, was from the beginning a road of suffering and humiliation, and the point of deepest humiliation was the point closest to the day of God's victory. It was his unique ministry and not just his earthly life of which Jesus spoke when on the cross he said, "It is finished." The ministry of Jesus the Christ was finished. The triumph of God's love and truth and the conquest of the enemy were complete. No more needed to be done. No other sacrifice needed to be offered. And yet it was not the end. Beyond the cross was the resurrection, and with the resurrection and the outpouring of the Spirit the commissioning and empowering of the ministry of the church, or, more truly, the ministry of the risen Lord in and through his church.

The Ministry in Jesus' Disciples

The central principle, that the nature of the ministry is determined for all time by the ministry of Jesus Christ, is so simple and obvious that in a church that takes the Scriptures seriously one might expect to be able to take it for granted. The Synoptic Gospels set clearly before us that Jesus expected his disciples to share his ministry, as servants with a master, it is true, yet also as friends in closest communion with him. When he sent them out into the towns and villages of Galilee, they were to preach the same gospel of the Kingdom that he was preaching; they were to proclaim to men the forgiveness of their sins as he himself was doing; also, like him, they were to take to men a healing of soul and body and liberation from the demonic forces of inner darkness that tyrannized over them. When Jesus trained the Twelve, it was not for some secondary ministry different in kind from his own; it was for participation with him in the only ministry he knew. But before they could share his ministry with him, there had to be a sharing on a yet deeper and more decisive level; the barriers in their inmost being, between Jesus and themselves, had to go down so that he could become the life within their life and they could become so one with him that they participated in some measure in the life that he had with God. John's Gospel dwells on this again and again, that the life of God, which was incarnate in Jesus Christ, became the life also of his disciples, and that the Spirit of God, which dwelt in all his fullness in Jesus Christ, took up his dwelling place in the disciples and created Christ afresh in them. The love of God in him had to become the love of God in them. The Acts of the Apostles also bears witness that what makes the church truly the church of Jesus Christ is the impartation to it of the same Spirit whose mighty works had been seen in Jesus' ministry. The church's possession of the Spirit is only a shadow of Jesus' full possession of it, for there is so much in a human church that blocks and resists God. We are left in no doubt that the New Testament church, in spite of its possession of the Spirit, was no perfect church but was characterized by a very human blindness and sinfulness. And yet with it and through it Jesus Christ wrought far greater triumphs among men than he ever knew in the years of his earthly ministry.

If it were not for the plain words of Jesus and his apostles in the New Testament, it would seem to us almost blasphemy to set the divine Lord and a human ministry in such close relation. It is startling that Jesus, who, whether he said it of himself or had it said of him by John, is uniquely " the light of the world " (John 8:12), is reported by Matthew to have said of his disciples what they would never have dared to say of themselves: " You are the light of the world " (Matt. 5:14). Surely it is this same continuity of ministry which is reflected in the words, " As the Father has sent me, even so send I you " (John 20:21; cf. Luke 10:16). He who was himself the great Fisher of Men, casting the net of his word into the sea of humanity to catch men and women for the life of his Kingdom, called his disciples to take up this same occupation and "become fishers of men" (Mark 1:17). Parallel to this is his conferring upon them the power of the keys. (Matt. 16:18.) It is a gross misunderstanding of Jesus' words to interpret the keys as though they referred to a power of admitting or excluding men at the gate of heaven or to some administrative function. The power of the keys is the power that Jesus himself was already exercising; in his word resided the power to open wide the gate of God's Kingdom to man in his need; but the word that was an open door to one man was a closed door to another. The word that took the publican and the sinner into the Kingdom shut the Pharisee out. A disciple in speaking this same word would exercise this same power, but not independently, for his word had power only in so far as it was the word of the same gospel.

Jesus tried to warn his disciples that if they were to share his ministry with him, they would also have to share his battle against the powers of evil and suffer with him in that battle. This would be the supreme test of their discipleship. When he sent the Seventy out on their mission, he conceived their expedition as an assault upon the forces of evil that held men enchained, and the report of their success drew from him the exclamation, "I saw Satan fall like lightning from heaven" (Luke 10:18). We think also of his words spoken in contemplation of his death: "Now shall the prince of this world be cast out" (John 12:31). His cross was the final crisis in the battle with evil. There the evil that enslaves man was unmasked and defeated; there Jesus Christ triumphed once and for all over the dark forces that are hidden in the unconquered self of man. But already in his ministry he was battling those same forces, and to share his ministry both before and after his death was to share with him the bruises and the agony of the battle.

The Last Supper has at its heart a testimony to the unity of Jesus with his disciples. Facing the prospect of death within a matter of hours, Jesus knew that the future rested with these muddled and sadly unready disciples. There is an infinite pathos in this final action of his in which he concentrates the entire meaning of his ministry. He breaks bread into pieces, and, giving it to them to eat, says to them, "This is my body." The word "body" in Hebrew psychology means the whole person, the self, so that what Jesus is saying is: "This is myself. Take me into your very being as you take this bread into your bodies that I may live in you." This was his provision for the continuation and completion of the redemptive work he had begun, a fellowship of disciples who, in spite of their human sinfulness and weakness, would let him be their life and continue his ministry in them and through them. He did not commission them to carry forward his ministry on their own. Rather, the possibility of it lay in his promise to them: "Lo, I am with you always, even unto the end of the world." It is not their ministry on his behalf but rather his ministry in them.

It is impressive that this same conception of the ministry appears in the letters of Paul. Paul likens the relation between the church and Jesus Christ to the relation between body and head in the human person. (I Cor., ch. 12.) The head rules the body, yet the body is necessary to the head, and both are united in the most intimate way. The living Christ, from the right hand of God in the unseen, rules the church, which is his body in the visible world; and its ministry is his ministry. A second likeness that Paul uses is that of husband and wife. The church is the bride of Christ, for whom he has been willing to die and who responds to his love with unconditional devotion. Like husband and wife, Christ and the church are bonded into the most intimate unity. It is this deep unity to which Paul bears witness when he speaks of being " in Christ " and of having Christ in him. These expressions have been interpreted by some scholars as a " Christ-mysticism " and as pointing to certain exalted experiences that came to Paul from time to time. Undoubtedly Paul had many ecstatic spiritual experiences, but it was something much more concrete and applicable to all Christians that Paul had in mind when he said, " Christ lives in me." It was not an inner, mystical experience but rather the daily ministry that he exercised among his fellow men that made him lay claim to such oneness with Christ. When he preached, it was not Paul but Christ who pleaded with men; when he healed the sick, it was Christ's hand that touched them through him; when he proclaimed the forgiveness of sins, men received it as Christ's word of forgiveness; and the secret joy of his most brutal sufferings was his consciousness that he was being counted worthy to share Christ's sufferings with him. There seems even to have been an idea at work in Paul's mind that in many ways the very events of Jesus' ministry were being reproduced in his own ministry. When he set out on his last journey to Palestine, he was convinced that, like Jesus, he was going up to Jerusalem to die.

The ministry of Jesus as it is continued in the apostles has two aspects: it is the establishment of the church's ministry for all time, revealing to us the character of that ministry when it is fulfilled not in the flesh of Jesus of Nazareth but in the flesh of sinful creatures like ourselves; but it is also the establishment in the apostles of a ministry that was to be the criterion by which the church of all the centuries should measure its ministry. It may be asked why this should be so, why the apostolic formulation of the Christian faith and of the ministry should have a validity superior to that of any later formulation, when the church of later times and even of our own times may be as truly the body of Jesus Christ as the church of the apostles. We cannot answer this challenge by idealizing the early church and representing it as perfect in all things and therefore to be imitated without question. It is only too clear that in the first half century of the church's history there were wide variations in the interpretation of the faith and in the order of the church's life. The Judaistic Christianity of the church of James was not identical with the Christianity of the Gentile churches of Paul. And if we can judge the character of Alexandrian Christianity by the report concerning Apollos in Acts 18:24 ff. and by later developments in Egypt, it was very different from either of the others. These variations seem to go back to a very early date, so that we cannot explain the authority of the apostolic church merely by pointing to its chronological proximity to the original events of revelation. There was no preservation of an inerrant tradition in the first generation of Christians merely by their closeness to Jesus Christ in time. Errors that were to cause the church great difficulty and were to be the source of serious division were already present among the original disciples. It is not any innate superiority of Peter to Luther or of Paul to John Wesley that causes us to subordinate Luther and Wesley to Peter and Paul. It could even be true that Luther was a better Christian than Peter and Wesley a better Christian than Paul.

The authority of the apostles does not reside in their personal character or in the quality of their Christian piety or in their possession of a supernatural wisdom that enabled them to be inerrant in all that they said and did, but solely in their function as witnesses to Jesus Christ — to his gospel, to his person, to his ministry. He committed himself to them in a way that marks them out from all other Christians. First, he gave them himself, taking possession of their very being, so that never again could they draw a breath without drawing it in a relation of oneness with him. They received him in direct personal confrontation, whereas all other Christians for all time can receive him only in indirect confrontation, through the witness of the apostles. Secondly, he committed to them his gospel, a gospel inseparable from his person, and so in them guarded against misinterpretation, since for them it could never become a set of impersonal doctrines and practices. Thirdly, he committed to them his ministry, and it was because of their immediate relation with him and his with them that the ministry in them was, in spite of all their human misunderstandings and cultural involvements, the uniquely genuine reflection and representation of his own ministry. It is simple historical fact that no one in all time has stood in the same relation with Jesus Christ as the original apostles. Nor is their function as apostles transferable. Their gospel, their faith, their ministry, can and must be shared by any church that is to be truly Christian, but not their apostleship. They retain their authority through all time as those to whom, because of their unique relation with Jesus Christ, we must ever go in order to receive our ministry. Since we meet them only through the Scriptures, their authority becomes for us the authority of the Scriptures, but actually it is not theirs in any personal sense at all but is simply the authority of God in Jesus Christ making itself manifest in their witness to him. Therefore, their human weaknesses and imperfections do not set in question the authority of the ministry that is fulfilled in them. The earthen vessel does not detract from the richness of the treasure (II Cor. 4:7) but serves rather to guard that, even where the ministry is the ministry of apostles, all the power and the glory should belong to God and not to men.

THE BROKENNESS OF THE CHURCH'S RELATION WITH JESUS CHRIST

The unity of Jesus' ministry with that of his apostles is so decisively attested in the New Testament that many churchmen and scholars fail to recognize that there is also a New Testament wit-

ness to discontinuity between the apostles and Jesus. The traditional doctrine of the church as the extension of the incarnation
in unbroken unity with Jesus Christ is the consequence of this
one-sidedness. The form in which it meets us in the work of many
present-day scholars is in the assertion that the term " Christ "
includes both Jesus and his apostles; so intimate was their unity
with him that the " Christ-event " comprehends the total revelation in Jesus of Nazareth and in the apostolic church. The resurrection of Jesus and the receiving of the Holy Spirit are then
regarded as indistinguishable, being merely two ways of expressing the church's consciousness of the presence of its Lord with
it and in it. Christology and ecclesiology merge into one.

We may well ask what the apostles themselves would have
thought of the disregard of essential distinctions entailed by this
doctrine. They have left behind a clear testimony to discontinuity
as well as to unity between themselves and Jesus Christ. They
represent themselves as misunderstanding and resisting the ministry for which he claimed them. They deliberately preserved
Jesus' words concerning them, that they knew not what manner
of spirit they were of (Luke 9:55). Jesus was the incarnation of
God; they received God in his Spirit to dwell in them but in such
incompleteness that they had each day to pray, " Come, Holy
Spirit." Jesus was sinless; they were sinners who were being sanctified and purified by the grace of their Lord. Jesus was God's
new man in whom God reigned triumphantly in each moment
of his existence; they were new men in and through Christ, but
in them a work of redemption had yet to be completed before
they would be like him. There was always the painful contrast
between Jesus' perfect obedience and their disobedience. In short,
there was a double truth concerning their existence as Christians:
by grace they were built into Christ as branches into a vine, so
that his life and strength and ministry became theirs; but as sinful human creatures they had constantly to confess themselves
unfaithful in their calling, branches broken from the vine and
in need of restoration. Anders Nygren, in his Laidlaw Lectures,
Christ and His Church (The Westminster Press, 1956, p. 92), uses

the parable of the vine and the branches as evidence that, as the branches are included in the vine, so the disciples are included within the Christ. This identification is open to serious misunderstanding and has far-reaching consequences for the doctrine of the church.

The ascension of Jesus is important at this point, in its position between the resurrection appearances and Pentecost. It is significant that when the story of the ascension is dismissed as merely an explanation of how the Christ who could appear in bodily form to men on earth became the exalted Christ at the right hand of the Father, not only does there cease to be any real distinction between the risen Lord and the Holy Spirit but also, what is even more important, the line begins to grow dim between the ministry of Jesus and the ministry of the apostles. Then the distinction between the ministry of the apostles and the subsequent ministry of the church becomes equally indistinct. The account of the ascension, in spite of its disturbing mythological features, may contain within it an essential witness to the uniqueness of the revelation of God in the ministry of Jesus Christ as known in his earthly life and death and in his resurrection. In that period the disciples had immediate knowledge of their Lord, and the authority of an apostle in the early church depended upon participation in that immediate knowledge. To have known Jesus Christ through the witness of others and through the Holy Spirit was not sufficient for an apostle. Paul's claim to apostleship was *not* based on his receiving of the Holy Spirit but on the extraordinary grace by which " as one born out of due time " he was given immediate knowledge of his Lord by a resurrection appearance like that which made others apostles. The ascension says that that immediate way of knowing Jesus Christ, so decisive for the faith of the disciples and for the creation of the church, came to an end, and even to the disciples in the new era that began at Pentecost he was known only mediately through the remembrance of him and the indwelling presence of the Holy Spirit. The era of the church was not just a continuation of the era of Jesus' earthly ministry, death, and resurrection. The second period, the era of the church, was wholly dependent upon the first, the era of primary witness, for its knowledge of Jesus Christ. The time of the church was the time between the ascension and the Second Coming, a time in which there would always be a contradiction between what the church was in Christ and what it was empirically. By grace, and only by grace and by " God's mercy " (II Cor. 4:1), it continues to be the body of Christ in which he lives and speaks and acts. It dare not therefore make grace something that it possesses *simpliciter,* without an ever-renewed repentance and restoration. It does not despair at being a sinful, imperfect church; it cannot despair, because it lives in hope of what it is yet to be by the grace of its Lord.

The apostolic ministry, then, in which the Christian ministry receives its decisive formulation, is simply the ministry of Jesus Christ being continued, expanded, and carried ever farther afield in the world as Jesus Christ lives and speaks and acts redemptively through his ministers. We must guard against the misunderstanding that would make of this an imitation of Jesus' earthly ministry as though we were committed merely to do and say and think what Jesus did and said and thought. Jesus' situation is not our situation. He attended the synagogue and observed religious practices that belonged to the Judaism of the first century. He dressed in the manner of a Palestinian. He employed in some respects the thought-forms of the rabbis. In short, he lived and spoke in the human situation of his time. We live in a different time, in a different situation, and in a very different thought-world. To imitate Jesus or the apostles laboriously in the form of our ministry today would be merely to produce an anachronism. We are not asked to do that. We are asked to submit our ministries to his that he may fulfill his ministry in us. Our unity with Jesus Christ is not an external uniformity but rather a unity in the Word and Spirit. The apostles in the book of The Acts do not repeat Jesus' sermons; their gospel is the same gospel that he preached, but, in the new situation created by his death and resurrection, they take the responsibility of finding new ways of expression for the gospel. In order to speak the same word that he spoke, they are compelled to use different words from those which he used. That becomes particularly clear when the apostles begin to preach to a Greek world that requires a radically new terminology. The repetition of Jesus' words would not have been an adequate proclamation of his gospel. It will perhaps make this statement more pointed if we imagine the situation had there been tape recorders in New Testament times. If a recording of Jesus' sermons and addresses had been made, would it then have been sufficient for the church through all time merely to keep playing over and over the words of Jesus with appropriate translations appended? The answer is, " No." The church in every age has to face the task of finding for itself the words and actions that will be a living embodiment of the Word and Spirit of Jesus Christ and the means whereby he may not only speak but also act in our midst today.

The Wholeness of Our Ministry

What, then, are the implications of this continuity between the ministry of Jesus Christ, the ministry of the apostles, and our ministry? Succeeding chapters will attempt to answer that question, but perhaps before all else it should impress upon our minds the inseparableness of the functions of the ministry. In fulfilling his ministry, Jesus was preacher, teacher, and pastor. The question may be asked why these three functions were not included in the analysis of the characteristics of Jesus' ministry. They belong, however, in a different category. The " characteristics " had to do with the nature of his ministry at a deeper level while these three functions are, rather, the forms in which that ministry found expression. *All* the characteristics that belong to the nature of the ministry are present in each of its forms of expression. In all three, Jesus is the shepherd seeking the lost, the herald of the Kingdom, the servant of all. So also does Paul exercise diverse functions in his ministry — preaching, teaching, pastoral care, administration, and a host of other duties. The suggestion is frequently heard that we have reached the age of specialization in the ministry: it is too much to expect a man to be a pastor as well as a preacher, and he should choose between teaching and preaching; no man can do more than one thing well. Harry Emerson Fosdick, in an article in *The Atlantic Monthly* in 1929, envisaged the church of the future as a series of large central institutions, each with a panel of ministers representing the various functions of the ministry. But the experience of the last thirty years leads us to see certain dangers in that direction. A preacher who accepts no responsibility for teaching or pastoral work is not likely to know what happens to his words in the lives of his people. On the other hand, teaching divorced from preaching tends to fall into legalistic and moralistic patterns. And pastoral counseling that is cut adrift from the work of preaching and teaching is in danger of losing its Christian character and becoming a kind of amateur psychiatry. The various functions of the ministry are necessary to each other, and one of the urgent needs of our day is the recovery of wholeness in our ministries. The man who tells himself that he has not time for all three major functions had best set down on paper what the things are for which he has time and to which he is giving priority over these essential aspects of a Christian ministry.

The centrality of preaching in the ministry of Jesus and the apostles is not difficult to recognize. Paul says, " Christ sent me not to baptize, but to preach the gospel." The command of the risen Christ to all the apostles is to preach the gospel in all the world. And from the moment that Jesus began his ministry in Galilee until he finished it on the cross he was constantly preaching. Not always was his preaching to a large audience; sometimes it was to a small group or even to a single person. And he used a variety of approaches to secure a hearing for it. When the congregations in the synagogues became weary of his message, he went out to the people who needed him and preached to them wherever he could find them. He knew that many of his words fell on stony soil or among the thorns, but he kept on preaching in confidence that some seed was falling in ready soil and God in his own good time would give the increase. The church today seems at times to be of uncertain mind about the centrality of preaching. And certainly preaching that does not dare to speak God's word after him, that does not attempt to be the instrument of God's revelation of himself in the contemporary situation, has no right at the center of Christian worship.

Jesus' ministry is also a teaching ministry. It is impossible to draw a sharp line between his preaching and his teaching. Yet they are two and not one. There is preaching and there is teaching. Jesus was not content when people responded to his call to repentance and faith and committed themselves to a new life. Such people, however genuine their faith, required care and teaching if they were to grow to their full spiritual stature. Jesus was not interested in having a host of loosely attached followers who would profess belief in him and a general loyalty to his way of life but nothing more; he was interested in having disciples who would have a sufficient understanding of his gospel and endowment with his Spirit so that they could fulfill a ministry for him. A teaching ministry has as its goal a fellowship of ministering Christians, with their pastor as their guide and director. He does not keep his ministry as his exclusive privilege, but, in so far as he can, he shares it with the members of his congregation.

The ministry of Jesus is also a pastoral ministry. He went in search of the persons who needed him; he did not wait for them to come to him. And, in spite of the crowds that pressed upon him and made it necessary for him to get up before daybreak in order to have time for prayer, he seems always to have had time for individuals who needed his ministry.

But prior to these forms of Jesus' ministry was his ministry of suffering. To him, with his knowledge of what prophets had had to face in the past, it was no surprise that to serve God unconditionally was to suffer, because such service had to be rendered in a human context where powerful forces were at work in opposition to God. " The world will hate you because you are not of the world." Jesus had only to cast his mind back over the whole line of the prophets from Moses to Second Isaiah to see that the service of God and suffering were inseparably linked. He counted the cost of his own ministry in suffering, and he warned his disciples of what the cost would be to them. But there is nothing stoic in Jesus' approach to suffering. He does not steel himself to endure it. Rather, he finds a divine purpose even in the suffering, and he takes it into himself in such a way that it bonds him together with a suffering humanity and at the same time becomes a force in him that breaks through the defenses of a blind and sinful humanity. He suffers with men and for them, and it is this which gives his words and his person their entry with men. He speaks to them and comes to them as one who has taken their burden of suffering into his own soul and bears it for them. It is the cross, therefore, that tells us what comes first in our ministry. Before our words or deeds can have any real and decisive significance for men, we have in some measure to have begun to suffer with them, to have put ourselves in their place, and to have felt the pain of their anxieties and distresses and guilt. If we are unwilling to suffer, we can neither preach nor teach nor be pastors to our people.

It is this ministry of Jesus, the Christ of God, into which we are called to enter. Its primary character is defined for us in him and in his chosen apostles. We have constantly to be inquiring of each of the four Evangelists and of the other New Testament writings concerning the nature of Jesus' ministry with the full consciousness that his ministry as depicted by them is both a judgment upon all our ministries and the promise of their only true effectiveness.

2

THE CHRISTIAN MINISTRY
IN THE LIGHT OF THE OLD TESTAMENT

IT is characteristic of books on the Christian ministry that they tend to ignore the Old Testament as though it had no significance for the formulation of the church's ministry. One exception is Thomas F. Torrance's *Royal Priesthood* (Alec Allenson, 1955), which contains much of interest and value but has the peculiarity that it makes the priesthood central to both the Old and the New Testaments. The thesis is advanced that most of the prophets were actually priests and that their prophetic utterances of God's word were merely an enlargement of the priestly function of giving Torah. The denunciation of ritual by Jeremiah and others was actually priestly criticism of priests. Second Isaiah is called a cult prophet in spite of his passionate antipathy to the sacrificial cult (Isa., ch. 66)! On this basis the prophetic writings are almost all comprehended within the priestly category with a consequent enhancement of its importance. The thesis, however, breaks down under its own weight for lack of any adequate foundation. The solidity of the prophetic tradition in the Old Testament cannot be so lightly absorbed into the priestly. The relation between prophets and priests was certainly closer than has been usually conceived. A. R. Johnson, in *The Cultic Prophet in Ancient Israel,* has demonstrated the possibility that the cult prophet may have been an official of a sanctuary and in close association with priests, but his theory rests on slender evidence and is only a possibility. No Old Testament scholar, however, has questioned that there were prophets *and* priests, and few would be likely to give the priestly tradition precedence over the prophetic. It is true that in Judaism the priestly element in the Old Testament predominated and the prophetic became much less significant. The scribes, or rabbis, have sometimes been represented as replacing the prophets on a different level, but actually they took over not the prophetic role but rather the priestly function of giving Torah, or instruction in sacred things, to the people. Thus in Judaism the two priestly duties of Torah and sacrifice were split apart, so that the priestly tradition had double representation, the prophetic falling away unrepresented, with serious results for the character of Judaism. In the scribal and rabbinic activity we have perhaps a suggestion of what was involved in the priestly giving of Torah, something quite different from the prophetic declaration of a word from God. With the advent of John the Baptist, then of Jesus, the prophetic tradition was reborn and recaptured the precedence that it had lost for centuries. It is against this background, perhaps, that one has to evaluate each new attempt to subordinate the prophetic to the priestly.

There are three distinct ministries in the Old Testament — prophetic, priestly, and kingly — and all three are essential to the covenant relation of Israel with God. Each comes to its fulfillment in Jesus Christ, fulfillment in the sense of being taken up and incorporated into the ministry of Jesus himself in such a way as to come to its full significance.

In Jesus' life, death, and resurrection we see the true meaning of prophet, priest, and king. Thus, if we are to enter into Jesus' ministry, we must, together with him, become prophets, priests, and kings. J. J. Von Allmen, in *Diener Sind Wir* (1958), interprets the functions of prophet, priest, and king as corresponding to the three aspects of ministry: preaching, teaching, and pastoral care. This neat correspondence of the two triads is tempting but fallacious. It obscures the fact that the whole of the ministry is present in each of its forms of expression. Preaching is prophetic but also priestly and kingly, and so also are teaching and pastoral care. In short, the three lines of Old Testament ministry run through

Jesus Christ into the ministry of the church, being fulfilled and illumined as they pass through him, but nevertheless in the meaning that he in his own person gives them remaining determinative for the nature of the church's ministry.

The Divorce of the Church from the Old Testament and Its Consequences

It is not surprising that the Old Testament has had so little part in contemporary thinking about the ministry when we realize to what a degree the Old Testament was torn apart from the New in the thinking of the church until very recently, both in the highest levels of theology and in the general practice of church members. Protestant orthodoxy in the seventeenth and eighteenth centuries asserted the unity of the two Testaments in such a way that the Sabbath law of Leviticus had an authority almost equal to any word or act of Jesus Christ, and Christianity was threatened with reversion to what was little more than a Christianized form of Judaism. In reaction to that false assertion of the unity of the Testaments, nineteenth-century rationalist and idealistic theology asserted the radical discontinuity between the two Testaments, emphasizing the great differences between the religion of the Old Testament and Christianity. Because this latter stream of theology was closely associated with the development of historical critical studies, the predominant viewpoint in Biblical scholarship in the nineteenth and early twentieth centuries was unfriendly to the assertion of more than a superficial unity between the two Testaments. The Old Testament might be represented as containing the records of the earlier stages of a religious development that came to its climax in the New, but any attempt to find theological unity between the two was viewed with distrust. We need to remember in the background the figures of Hegel, Schleiermacher, and Harnack. Hegel scorned the Old Testament as the embodiment of ideas directly opposed to his eternal and absolute truths. Schleiermacher found elements in every part of the Old Testament that were inconsistent with Christian piety, and suggested that it would be less open to misunderstanding and misuse if the Old Testament were printed as an appendix to the New instead of preceding it. Harnack openly advocated the abandonment of the Old Testament as canonical Scripture on the grounds that its whole approach to religion is inconsistent with the New Testament gospel.

This divorce between the Testaments is by no means a thing of the past. The wide gulf between Old and New Testament scholarship is still distressingly wide in spite of the attempts that are being made to bridge it. Very few books on the New Testament take the Old Testament seriously as being important for the understanding of the New. And there are still many Old Testament scholars who would rebel at the statement that the Old Testament is never rightly understood until it is read in the light of its fulfillment in the New. But perhaps today we are beginning to see that both continuity and discontinuity must be asserted if we are to understand the relation between the Testaments. The church in setting them together in a single canon of Scripture bore witness to the fact that both were necessary to God's revelation of himself to man; and, in keeping them separate, it left with us the warning that they must be read as two and not one, as promise and fulfillment, without confusing the era of promise with the era of fulfillment.

We must not think, however, that this divorce between the Testaments has taken place only on the level of Biblical and theological scholarship. It is manifest on every hand in the life of the church. In the year 1934 in the days of Hitler in Germany the proposal was made by the German-Christian party in the Protestant church that the Old Testament should be removed from the Christian Scriptures. The proposal had behind it more than the immediate anti-Semitism of the Nazi movement; it was the expression of a long-standing alienation of the church from the Old Testament. American Christians, reading in the newspapers what was proposed, were shocked. But there was an element of unconscious hypocrisy in that reaction, for here also in America there is an alienation of the membership of the church from the Old Testament. In fact, it has so completely lost its significance for many people that, if it were removed from their Bibles and blank pages substituted to maintain the normal appearance of the book, they might not notice its disappearance for some years. But perhaps this unawareness of the Old Testament is the consequence of the rarity with which congregations have heard sermons that take the Old Testament seriously as Christian Scripture out of which one preaches the Christian gospel. Fragments of the prophets that have a social emphasis may be heard occasionally. The psalms provide texts for sermons on the devotional life. But, in general, the Old Testament has become largely a closed book in the church.

This divorce of the church from the Old Testament has had serious consequences in the church's understanding both of itself and of its ministry. We do not have to read far in church history to discover that the Old Testament has been more than once the bulwark of the church against the Hellenizing of its gospel and its character. As the church made its way in the Graeco-Roman world, the interpretation of its gospel in the language of that world brought gradually a substitution of Greek philosophical ideas in place of Christian ones. The words " God," " man," and " world " were given something of the meaning they had long had in the Greek world rather than the meaning that they had for Jesus and Paul. These Greek meanings were superimposed upon the New Testament with some measure of success, but there was no success in superimposing them upon the Old Testament. In the Old Testament the antithesis between Greek and Hebraic ways of thinking stands out with starkness. Therefore Marcion, in the second century, made his proposal that the Old Testament be abandoned by the church. So also in the nineteenth century the idealist philosophers and theologians could read their ideas into the New Testament, but the Old Testament resisted them so stubbornly that they could make nothing of it. The Old Testament is like a crude guardian of the gospel whom we dismiss at our peril; and it is not difficult to establish that the neglect of the Old Testament in the church has left the door open for all manner of gospels to come wandering in, most of them products of the same Greek humanist tradition that imperiled the church in earlier eras.

Our interest, however, is centered upon the ministry. We want to know what consequences the neglect of the Old Testament has had upon the church's ministry. Just as with the gospel itself, the ministry tends to be interpreted in idealistic terms rather than in direct line with what is to be traced in the Scriptures. The minister is the servant of " truth in general " rather than of any specific Biblical revelation of truth. Christian truth is just the central core of " truth in general." The minister is the enlightened man to whom people come for enlightenment; therefore, he has a right to set himself at the center of the church's life. It is from him that the community draws continually the strengthening and clarification of its ideals and guidance toward their realization. The ministry is understood largely as something a man does for his fellow men. He helps them toward a truer and more intelligent outlook on life. He encourages them in the struggles and difficulties of their daily existence. He points out to them their responsibilities and duties. But no longer does he exercise the prophetic, priestly, or kingly functions of the Biblical ministry, all of which were focused primarily upon man's relation with God. He would never think of making the prophetic claim for his preaching that it is God's word to his people. He does not consider his function as in any way priestly, that is, representative of his people with God. And the idea of a kingly authority residing in the ministry, superior to the authority of all earthly rulers, is utterly inconceivable to him. We must, therefore, undertake now to show that the ministry of Jesus contains within it the prophetic, priestly, and kingly ministries and that, where they are absent, the ministry of the church has lost its essential Christian character.

A NATION CHOSEN TO MINISTER

The background of a doctrine of the ministry in the Old Testament is the doctrine of election, the election of Israel, which in Christian terms is the doctrine of the church. It is not so long since Christian theologians were embarrassed by the stubborn

insistence of the Old Testament that Israel from its earliest beginnings was God's chosen people, marked out by him for a
destiny different from that of any other nation. This seemed to
be a primitive idea, inconsistent with the New Testament doctrine of God's care over all nations. Seeming parallels to it were
found in other nations, in the conviction of kings such as Tiglath-
pileser and Cyrus that they were the chosen of the gods. It was
interpreted as an expression of the natural pride of nation and
race. But more recent study of the concept of election, such as it
has received at the hands of the Continental scholars Eichrodt
and von Rad, or in a volume by the English scholar H. H. Rowley,
in 1950 (*The Biblical Doctrine of Election*), finds in it no such
primitiveness. To Rowley the call of Israel is directly parallel
with the call of Moses or Amos or Isaiah or Jeremiah. In fact, the
call of the individual prophet expresses in miniature the meaning
of God's call to the nation. Israel was chosen for service, that is,
for ministry, to be the instrument of God's purpose in the world.
The full implications of this call to Israel were not immediately
apparent in the Mosaic Age, and through the centuries there was
a constant temptation to interpret Israel's chosenness as a basis for
expecting special privileges and advantages from God. But it was
the function of the prophets again and again to puncture such
pretentions and to recall Israel to its unique destiny.

The high point in the prophetic interpretation of the doctrine
of election is in Isa., chs. 40 to 66, where Second Isaiah urges on
his scattered people their missionary destiny as the servant people
of God. The destruction of Jerusalem and the shattering of their
national life have cleared the way for them to lay hold at last upon
God's original purpose in bringing them into being, that through
them the light of his truth may shine out into all the earth and all
men may find the answer to their need in him. There is evidence
that the prophet was disappointed in his dream. Even after the
discipline of exile the nation was not ready for such a high conception of its destiny. Yet there was a remnant gathered round
the prophet who affirmed with him this destiny and dreamed with
him of a time when all God's people would be priests and proph-

ets of God. The first thing, therefore, that we have to say concerning the ministry in Israel is that it belonged primarily and in principle to the nation as a whole. The basic meaning of Israel's existence was ministry, the service of God, the setting at God's disposal of human agencies through which he might work in order to effect the redemption of the world. It is not just Moses and Elijah and Amos and Jeremiah who are called into a ministry. All Israel is called, and individual ministries are on behalf of Israel as a whole, just as in the Christian church the ministry belongs to the whole church as the body of Christ and individual ministries are on behalf of the church as a whole.

Here already we touch upon a principle that is of the highest importance in our day. Is the ministry the exclusive prerogative and responsibility of an ordained clergy, so that ordinary Christians are not expected to have any share in it? Hendrik Kraemer, in *A Theology of the Laity* (The Westminster Press, 1958), points out how recently the church has begun to comprehend the implications of the election of all Israel to ministry. The Reformers, in spite of their doctrine of the priesthood of all believers, went only part way in recognizing the ministry of the ordinary Christian. Significant work in this regard is being done by the Department on the Laity of the World Council of Churches. Whatever our official doctrine may be, consciously or unconsciously the idea that the ministry is the exclusive responsibility of ordained clergy is prevailing in our churches. The ordinary Christian no longer considers himself called to a ministry. Only clergy and special church workers are so called. All others have their lives as Christians on a different level. Why do so few church members feel any urgency about special training that would deepen their understanding of the Christian faith and equip them to be active, coherent disciples? It is because they are content to be what they call "just ordinary Christians," who do not need ever to open their mouths on any subject that has to do with the Christian faith. The Roman Church long ago codified this order, establishing two levels within the church and defining the clergy to which the ministry is assigned as alone representing the essence of the church. The fact that the Roman Church makes extensive use of laymen and women in secondary ministries, some of them becoming distinguished theological teachers, does not alter the basic separation. We do not realize how much the actual order in our churches has been drifting toward the Roman pattern. It is significant, therefore, that both Old and New Testaments are agreed that there is a ministry that belongs to the whole people of God.

SPECIAL MINISTRIES IN ISRAEL

It is equally clear in the Old Testament that there would have been no Israel had it not been for special ministries. It is most likely a valid historical tradition that traces the origin of the nation to the decision of one man, Abraham, to leave behind the Chaldean civilization of Ur and to found a new people somewhere in the West. Then, had there been no Moses seeing his vision of God on the mountainside and taking up the arduous task of leadership, there would have been no exodus and no history of Israel. Had there been no Elijah fulfilling his prophetic ministry against great odds and bitter discouragements, the nation might well have sunk deeply into the sensuous mire of Baalism and disappeared completely from human history. And we shudder to think of what would have happened in the sixth century when the nation was broken and scattered to the four winds had it not been for the ministries of Jeremiah, Ezekiel, and Second Isaiah. God needed within Israel special ministries in order to maintain the covenant bond between Israel and himself. So also does God need special ministries within his church. He needs men and women who will form a channel of communication between him and his church, through whom he can speak ever afresh to his church and in whom the church will be itself constantly reminded of and recalled to its true destiny.

In the earliest examples of ministry in the Old Testament the three functions of prophet, priest, and king are combined. With Abraham it is difficult to say what is history and what is the reflection of a later faith; nevertheless, his portrait is an early record for us of what Israel understood by a man of God. There is a sense in which he incarnates Israel's conception of itself, called of God to a great destiny, confronted with fearful difficulties and uncertainties in the realization of that destiny, endangered by inner weaknesses, yet carried forward into the unknown by the promise of God. Abraham is no prophet in the manner of Moses or Elijah, and yet he performs the function of the prophet in being the man to whom God reveals his purpose. He belongs to no order of priesthood, yet he performs the function of a priest, offering sacrifices and interceding with God in prayer on behalf of others. He has no royal titles, yet within the narrow scope of his own small society he bears the responsibility of the chief executive.

In the person of Moses the three functions are much more clearly evident. Before all else Moses is the prophet of God to whom God reveals his mind and heart and through whom Israel is brought to a living knowledge of God. Moses is God's spokesman to Israel. But he is also Israel's priest before God. He goes alone into the sanctuary to offer prayers for Israel and to seek for them direction from God concerning all things in their life. Aaron, the priest, stands alongside him, yet Moses himself is represented more than once performing the duties of a priest. And Moses is king in all but the name. He rules in Israel, at first alone and then with the support of the elders. A third figure in whom the three functions are united is Samuel. Sometimes the fact that Samuel is the great kingmaker in the early stories of the kingdom conceals the degree of power that belonged to him in the immediately preceding period. Religious and political leadership came together in his hands, and religiously he is represented as both prophet and priest. The question may well be raised whether this combination of functions in these early figures of Israel's history is the consequence of a certain idealizing of them, making of them types of the Messiah who was yet to come in whom prophet, priest, and king would be perfectly united. It was characteristic of Israel's thinking to see the distant future reflected in the distant past.

After the time of Samuel the three aspects of ministry in Israel find each a separate development, although not so separate as has been sometimes thought. The antithesis of prophet and priest in the Books of Amos and Jeremiah misled scholars for a time, so that in sympathy with the prophets they passed whole-sale condemnations upon the entire priesthood of Israel. Adam Welch entered a protest against this in 1936 in his *Prophet and Priest in Old Israel,* and more recently Aubrey Johnson has demonstrated the close connection of some of the prophets with the places of worship in his *The Cultic Prophet in Ancient Israel.* Also the character of Deuteronomy and of the priestly document shows us that the priests made themselves custodians in Israel of many of the great insights of the prophets. We might also note the identity of high priest and civil ruler in later Jewish history. It is important that all three — prophet, priest, and king — were known as the " anointed of God," moshiach or messiah, and in the Qumrân sect the expectation was of at least two, and perhaps even three, messiahs, one prophetic, one priestly, and one royal.

It was the covenant relation of God with Israel that called for this threefold ministry. The covenant was not a legal relationship, as it has sometimes been represented. Rather, it was an intensely personal relationship, best likened to that between husband and wife in marriage. But in the covenant, God was sovereign and Israel was subject; not, however, in any servile way, for it was a sovereignty in love and a subjection in love. It was, as can be demonstrated in history and particularly in the biographies of the prophets, a subjection in which Israelites found a freedom and a mastery in life that were unique in the ancient world. God's absolute sovereignty within the covenant did not make slaves of Israelites but rather made free men of them, free in a way that other men had never known. The preservation of this personal covenant relation between God and Israel was the purpose of the threefold ministry.

The functions of prophet and priest within the covenant are very simply stated. In this personal relation with Israel God had to have someone to speak for him. It was in his love for his people that he said, " Whom shall we send, and who will go for us? " (Isa. 6:8), and a succession of men, such as Isaiah, overheard him and let themselves be called into this special service. Then, as Israel responded to God, this response pressed for expression in worship, and there was need of someone to perform the priestly office of standing as the people's representative before God, of inquiring for them concerning the will of God, then of offering their sacrifices to God and of treasuring all things that contributed to the deepening, stabilizing, and enriching of their relation with God. It should be emphasized that in pre-exilic Israel the primary duty of the priest was teaching and the general direction of cultic life. Not until after the exile did the offering of sacrifice take first place.

In the present day most persons would be inclined to regard only these two ministries as religious and as essential to the covenant relation, dismissing the third, that of the king, as a purely secular function. But not so in Israel. It is distinctive of the Old Testament faith that kingship in Israel was interpreted as a religious function, a ministry of God. Calvin and Luther understood this, and it is neither to our credit as a church nor a benefit to the health of the body politic that we have forgotten it and have denuded the state of its religious significance. In these days when the state has grown to such gigantic proportions, it needs as never before to be reminded that it can never possess the supreme and absolute authority, and that, when it acts as though it were answerable to no one beyond itself, it sins against God. In Israel the king was constantly reminded by his prophets, and by the liturgy of the sanctuary, that Yahweh alone was rightly king in this nation and that he who sat upon the throne for a time was exercising a ministry on God's behalf. The prophets saw this to be true even of foreign kings. This understanding of true kingship as a ministry in Israel is a sign that the sacred and secular are not to be cut apart into two isolated realms, that God's sovereignty extends over the whole of man's existence, and that in the life of the community, whether it be family, local, national, or international, there can be no soundness or health unless obedience to constituted authority is interpreted in some way as obedience to God. Rightly to digest this Old Testament doctrine would be to rethink the whole relationship of church and state in the American scene.

THE PROPHETIC MINISTRY

We must now attempt to define more carefully each of these three aspects of ministry within the covenant, remembering always that it is the Old Testament order that is before us and not the full stature of each, which it attains only in Jesus Christ. It will perhaps keep our perspective right if we glance ahead and remind ourselves that in Jesus Christ prophecy, priesthood, and kingship as ministries of God receive their ultimate definition. In the Old Testament we have, not fulfillment but promise — the promise, not just in words or dreams but in personal existences, of the ministry that by God's grace was yet to be established. The promise, however, must be held together with the fulfillment. We see what was fulfilled in Jesus Christ only when we also know what was promised.

The word "prophetic" has been debased in various ways. In some quarters the term "prophetic ministry" signifies one in which sermons on texts from the Books of Daniel and Revelation occur with great frequency, and from these books the secrets of future history are disclosed. At the opposite extreme are those to whom a prophetic ministry is one that concentrates largely upon attacking social evils and makes the gospel into a program for social reform. There is need for much more careful definition of the implications of the prophetic tradition for the Christian ministry.

A prophet is before all else a mediator. He is "sent from God." He stands between God and man with the responsibility of faithfully declaring to man what he has heard from God. To man in his rebellion against God this declaration takes the form of a warning of imminent judgment. But to the man who repents and turns to God with all his heart it is the promise of blessing and of a future in which God's justice and goodness will eventually triumph. The prophet recognizes the source of all disorder and evil in life in the rupture of the covenant relationship between God and Israel. Israel is truly Israel and man is truly man only in a relation of openness and trust toward God in which the justice, truth, and mercy of God are reflected in the life of his people as in a mirror. The destruction of this relation by Israel's blindness and sin has in it potentially the destruction of the nation, and the restoration of it has in it potentially the resurrection of the nation. In this situation the prophet is God's man, bonded together with God, so that God's purpose is his purpose and God's word his word, and yet at the same time bonded together with his nation, carrying upon his heart the burden of its sin and the peril of its situation, so that he feels in himself the agony of the judgment he proclaims. Jeremiah was not the only prophet who knew what it cost in suffering to be God's man in Israel. The Suffering Servant of Second Isaiah is a focusing of the experience of all the prophets. There could be no such mediation as they attempted without suffering. In the breach between God and man there was from the beginning the shadow of a cross.

It is against this background that we understand the prophet's "Thus saith the Lord." This is no mere mechanical formula that he prefixes to his remarks in order to claim divine authority for them. He speaks only that which he is convinced is the expression of the inmost heart and mind of God himself. Nowhere do we look more deeply into the inner life of a prophet than in Isa. 50:4, where the prophet says, "The Lord hath given me the tongue of a learner, that I should know how to speak a word in season to him that is weary: he wakeneth morning by morning, he wakeneth mine ear to hear as a learner." An ear open continually toward God to hear what he has to say to weary, broken, stumbling humanity and a tongue ready and disciplined to speak the cauterizing and healing words — that is the true portrait of the prophet.

Such a prophet speaks with authority because, even though he is familiar with the great prophetic tradition that lies behind him, he does not merely repeat the words of former prophets, but, helped by their insight, and standing in communion with them, he hears God's word for himself and speaks it directly into the contemporary situation. Never do we find a prophet mouthing eternal and timeless truths. Each word he speaks is a personal word from a personal God to actual men with whom He is deeply concerned. Here at once we are reminded of the authority of which men were aware in the words of Jesus. The rabbis who turned the personal word of the prophet into an impersonal law or an impersonal truth, to be supported by long quotations of Biblical and rabbinic authorities, stand in contrast not only to Jesus but also to the prophets. And yet the Christian ministry has not always been clear in which tradition it should stand and has at times been closer to the rabbinic than to the prophetic, the rabbinic seeming much more concrete than the prophetic, when in actuality it brought with it a disastrous loss in authority.

The prophet's relation to his people was that of a watchman or shepherd. Ezekiel uses both terms to express his conception of his office. In an ancient city with its protective walls and gates there had always to be a watchman upon the wall to give warning of any approaching enemy from without or peril from within. The prophet's warning cry was therefore an expression of his care for Israel, and the harshness of his words of judgment was a sign not of unloving anger but rather of the urgency of his alarm. It is thus an error to suggest, as some scholars have done, that Amos is a forbidding figure, all judgment and no mercy. The sharpness of his severity is the measure of his concern for Israel.

We are likely to find Ezekiel's image of the shepherd more congenial than that of the watchman, but it has actually the same content. The prophet as shepherd guards the flock night and day against harm from enemies, but he also guides the sheep by day to the sources of food and water. Both images of watchman and shepherd lay heavy responsibility upon the prophet. The shepherd is responsible to his master for the lives of his sheep, and the watchman is responsible for the safety of the city. Ezekiel says that the soul that dies without the prophet's warning will be laid to the charge of the prophet. Paul, in his last address to the Ephesian elders, took this up into his conception of the ministry: "I am pure from the blood of all men. For I have not shunned to declare unto you all the counsel of God" (Acts 20:26-27).

In calling the prophet a shepherd of souls we must not fall into a misconception of the soul that is widely prevalent but that differs radically from anything that would enter the mind of a prophet. Some modern shepherds of souls define the soul as a spiritual entity existing in detachment from the world. What is happening to men in the social, economic, and political spheres is regarded as a secular matter to be left to the social scientists, economists, and politicians and not to be touched by the minister. Any one of the prophets, and Jesus with them, would have been aghast at such a conception of man. Biblically the soul is defined as the total self of man. He does not have a soul; he *is* a soul. Inner and outer life are inseparable. Events in the market place, the courts, and the councils of the princes are an expression of the nation's soul. God is concerned with the total life of man and not just with some " spiritual " part of him. God claims sovereignty in all things. Therefore, the prophet as shepherd and watchman takes the entire life of the nation as the scope of his interest. It is important to point out the unity of the prophets with Jesus in this respect, for his ministry is often interpreted as wholly a ministry to individuals, or a " saving of *souls*." Why, then, did he go up to Jerusalem when there were plenty of individuals elsewhere who needed his ministry? And why did he limit his mission in his lifetime to the house of Israel? Jesus' ministry, though it focuses constantly upon individuals, does this within the context of a mission to the nation as a whole. He calls Israel to its historic destiny as the people of God and weeps over Jerusalem when the nation refuses to respond to his call.

Nothing takes us more directly to the heart of the prophet's faith than his conviction that God has a special care for the poor and hungry and helpless, the victims of injustice and oppression. The prophet is consistently their spokesman and defender. It may be the king himself who has been guilty of the wrong against his fellow man, but his royalty is no protection against the prophet. Fearlessly a Nathan or an Amos or a Jeremiah exposes the shame of the king and calls him to repentance. To postexilic Israel, Second Isaiah declares that unless the hungry are fed and the poor man has justice done to him, there is no reason to expect any mercy from God. God's mercy is only for the merciful. Here we find ourselves deep in the New Testament gospel where, in such parables as the good Samaritan and Dives and Lazarus, and in the depiction of the Last Judgment in Matt., ch. 25, Jesus made the test of faith to be whether or not a man had responded with compassion to the plight of his brother in distress.

As we describe the ministry of the prophets in such terms as these, it seems as though we were describing the ministry of Jesus himself. We become aware of how closely knit his mission is with that of the prophets. We understand the unity of Jesus with John the Baptist. Jesus fulfills the mission of the prophets in the sense that he brings to its completion the service of God begun in them. His ministry is a prophetic ministry, and we who enter into his ministry must share his oneness with the prophets or we are something less than Christian in our service of God. But Jesus is not just a prophet; he is the fulfillment of prophecy. He does what John the Baptist knew had to be done, though John himself could not do it: he baptizes men into God. In Jesus' own person, God comes to man and abides with him in the power of his indwelling Spirit. Jesus writes the law in men's hearts and so initiates the new covenant dreamed of by Jeremiah. The prophetic ministry thus finds its continuation and completion in a larger and deeper and more decisive ministry.

The Priestly Ministry

The priestly aspect of the ministry can be dealt with much more briefly. Our temptation in some parts of Protestantism is to ignore it entirely, quoting the denunciations of the priests and their ritual which are to be found in the writings of some of the prophets, and assuming that the Old Testament priestly tradition found no fulfillment in Jesus Christ. That can be a serious and crippling error. It is a misrepresentation of the priests of Israel. There were indeed false priests just as there were false prophets, but there were also true and faithful priests who took with great seriousness their sacred calling as representatives of Israel before God. If we examine the priestly document in the Pentateuch, we must be impressed with the way in which the priests conserved and interpreted the religious heritage of Israel, making themselves custodians of the records of God's dealings with his people. They took up into their thinking the contribution of the great prophets. The psalms take us into the ritual of the Temple, which was under the care of the priests, and it is some measure of the quality of their faith and of their theology that the worship of the Christian church today rests in a large measure upon foundations laid by them. We must not forget that the primary function of the priest in pre-exilic Israel was not the offering of sacrifice but leadership in worship and the instruction of the people in the knowledge of God. In the earlier period, sacrifice could be offered by others than priests, and only in post-exilic times, when scribes took over the duties of religious instruction, did sacrifice become the chief duty of the priest. The priest was the representative of Israel before God. In his prayers he sought to gather up the longings and desires of his people and also their reasons for thanksgiving and rejoicing before God. And on the Day of Atonement it must have been an awesome thing as he went into the Holy of Holies to secure forgiveness for the sins of the nation.

Already in the Old Testament there is a prophetic reinterpretation of sacrifice and priesthood. The true sacrifice is seen to be not the bloody offering upon the altar but rather the broken and contrite heart of the man who has been utterly humbled before God (Ps. 51:16-17; Isa. 66:1-3), the self-offering of him who has given himself unconditionally to the service of the Word (Isa. 53:10). The true temple is not one that men can build with wood and stone but a community of people who are ready and willing to follow at God's bidding (ch. 66:1-2). The true priesthood is this servant-people, anointed with God's Spirit (ch. 63:1), with his word upon their lips (ch. 49:2), and with the task of mediating God's Torah to all mankind (chs. 42:4; 49:6). Here the Old Testament itself points in the direction in which priesthood was to find its fulfillment, and it is significant that wherever in the New Testament the term " priesthood " is used it refers not to a special ministry but to the priestly function of the whole people of God.

It is important to note that there is a difference in the way in which priest and prophet come to fulfillment in Jesus himself. The marks of the prophetic ministry are plainly visible in the ministry of Jesus. In him, as in John the Baptist, the Old Testament prophet lives again as he had not been known for five hundred years. But we cannot say that in him the Old Testament priest lives again. Rather, it must be said that Jesus seems to have avoided deliberately any association with the priesthood of his day. His solidarity with the prophet John he acknowledged by being baptized by him and by publicly associating with him. But priest and Temple sacrifice seem to have held no interest for him. His parable of the good Samaritan paints a satirical picture of priest and Levite who, in obedience to ritual law, must avoid all possibility of contact with a dead body lest it unfit them for their duties in the sanctuary, and who therefore do not get close enough to the wounded man to recognize whether he is alive or dead. Though Jesus worshiped regularly in the synagogue, there is no word of him entering the Temple for worship after the age of twelve. This is not proof that he did not worship in the Temple. Attention may be drawn to the fact that Jerusalem Christians are represented as worshiping in the Temple in The Acts and that Jesus' cleansing of the Temple indicates his concern for it. But surely the absence of any reference to his worshiping in the Temple, while it is indicated that he was accustomed to worship regularly in the synagogue, has some significance. His cleansing of the Temple indicates his severely critical attitude toward the existing priesthood.

In The Letter to the Hebrews, and also to some extent in the writings of Paul, the language of priesthood and sacrifice is used to interpret the ministry of Jesus. It will be found upon close examination that in the main this is an interpretation that follows the pattern already marked out by Second Isaiah. Paul never uses the term " priest " to describe the ministry of the church — apostles, evangelists, pastors, teachers, healers, administrators, but not priests. But how could it be otherwise for a Hebrew when he tried to say what had been accomplished for all mankind by the self-offering of Jesus in his ministry and upon the cross, particularly if that Hebrew had been nourished upon the writings of Second Isaiah (as we know that the Essenes and the followers of John the Baptist were), than that he should see in Jesus the true priest offering once and for all the only sacrifice that can be acceptable to God, the sacrifice of his humility and perfect obedience? In Hebrews, Jesus is portrayed as the Great High Priest, who on our behalf has entered into the Holy of Holies in the heavens to secure for us our forgiveness. But he is not only high priest; he is also the sacrifice that is offered once and for all, by which we are restored in him to oneness with God.

The truth that this representation of Jesus' ministry embodies is of central significance. It focuses attention on his self-offering. More important than all his preaching and teaching was his suffering and self-giving, which began long before the Last Week, for it was by his sacrificial self-giving, obedient even unto death, that he purchased for himself a church. In his death he made himself our representative before God, took up into himself all our sin and shame and sorrow, and thereby lifted our life into the transforming presence of God where all things are made new.

Since there is this priestly and sacrificial character to Jesus' ministry at its climax, there must be a priestly and sacrificial element in our ministries, for our ministry is empty except it be filled from his, and we are nothing except in oneness with him. But when we consider what it is in Jesus' ministry that constitutes the priestly and sacrificial — namely, self-giving, self-offering, intercession, identification in love with man in his need, suffering for sinners even unto the death — we are guarded from thinking of priestliness as a formal, ritual, official, externally authoritative character that is assumed by the ministry. The priest knows that he must speak in God's name but that his words will have no power unless first he has identified himself with the man to whom he speaks, no matter what the cost. The priest will be kept from any display of his personal idiosyncracies in leading his people in worship, since he knows himself to be their representative and spokesman before God, so that not only in prayers but also in the reading of Scripture, in the Eucharist and in preaching, he will be one with them, offering himself with them to God and receiving with them the living Word, which is the bread of life. The priest has entered into the mystery of his Lord's sufferings and is not deterred from his ministry to mankind in its painful dilemmas by the knowledge that there is no mediation of Christ's forgiveness to man in the depth of his need without a sharing of Christ's agonizing concern for the sinner. But when the claim to priesthood becomes a claim to exclusive possession of priestly powers and office, glorifying a ritual sacrifice rather than the sacrifice of the broken and contrite heart, and seeking to imprison God in a human institution with clearly defined borders instead of acknowledging the fellowship of all true believers as his chosen dwelling place, then both " priest " and " sacrifice " have lost the meaning that was given them in the first Christian community.

The Kingly Ministry

The third aspect of the Old Testament ministry is the kingly. The king is represented everywhere in the Old Testament as a minister of God, a different kind of ministry from that of prophet or priest, nevertheless, God's minister. Saul and David were called of God to become kings. They were anointed not only with oil but with God's Spirit as a sign that they belonged to God. The person of the king was sacred, so that he who cursed him or laid violent hands on him sinned against God. We have coronation psalms preserved that speak of the king in such exalted terms that we shrink from the recognition that such language was used of a human king. But never is the king raised to the level of a God as he was in Egypt and Rome. He remains a man, an Israelite among Israelites, but called of God to the office of ruling Israel on God's behalf. Here the Israelites took the realities of political life with a much greater seriousness than we do, and they saw deeply into the problem of the relation of political power to God. God's sovereignty over all things meant God's sovereignty over the life of man in his political and economic affairs. There, as well as in the ostensibly religious aspects of his life, he was responsible to God, and to be cut off from God was to be delivered over to destruction.

This line of thought we now trace to its destination in Jesus Christ. The title " Messiah," or " Anointed One," was the title of all Israel's kings, but it had come to signify mainly the great King who one day would come to rule on God's behalf. It seems at first sight a most unsuitable title for the man of Nazareth in his simplicity and poverty, in his refusal to use any form of compulsion to effect his purpose, and finally in his helplessness and defeat upon the cross. This is no conquering King! But the unanimous testimony of the New Testament is that this *is* the conquering King, God's King come to set up his Kingdom in the midst of the world. He does not rule by compulsion from without, but nevertheless he rules, exerting a far more powerful compulsion from within.

Here also we must follow Jesus Christ in his ministry. He calls us to be not just priests but " kings and priests to God." There is a power over the lives of men that the minister of Christ must covet and cherish and exercise without fear. He must know that, in spite of all practical lines of separation between church and state, the rightful king in every land resides not in the houses of government but in the church, in so far as the church is in truth the body of the *Lord* Jesus Christ. Jesus Christ is King and Lord, not just over his church or over the spiritual life of his people (whatever that may mean), but over the total life of man. He exercises his rule through his church, not in such a way as to make the church a rival of the government (as has sometimes happened) but in such a way that men in all their affairs may know that they cannot find the true order of their life in any sphere except in obedience to the word of Jesus Christ. It is not presumption for the church and its ministry to claim such authority over the whole of life. Timidity here is unfaithfulness to our Lord. *He* is the One who claims this authority, and to be silent about his claim is to deliver up the world of human affairs to false lords in whom there is no salvation.

Jesus Christ is prophet, priest, and king, and we are his ministers only when we share with him his prophetic, priestly, and kingly functions.

3

THE MINISTRY OF THE WORD

WHEN we consider how important preaching and teaching were, not only to the prophet but also, in a minor form, to the priest in the pre-exilic period, and how much of the time of Jesus and his apostles was occupied with preaching and teaching, it is difficult to understand how either activity could ever be allowed to recede into the background in the life of the church. And yet there have been long periods when either or both of them have fallen into neglect. It may, however, be taken as axiomatic that a church that is in continuity with the church of the Scriptures can neglect neither preaching nor teaching. This statement requires some conditioning. It does not mean that the preparation of sermons to be preached from a pulpit is more important than the pastoral task of dealing with individuals, for the heart of the pastoral task may be an intimate and informal proclamation of the Gospel. Nor does teaching signify only the educational work that is carried on within the confines of the church building. Much of the preaching and teaching that we are able to observe in the Bible was not done from a pulpit or in a classroom but in a much wider variety of situations. Nevertheless, the Bible in a very large measure consists of the distillation of centuries of preaching and teaching. The book of Deuteronomy is a great powerful sermon to Israel, and so also are the books of Samuel and Kings when we think of them being read by a nation on which had come the disaster of the exile. The books of the prophets are almost wholly collections of their sermons. And the Synoptic Gospels, according to the interpretation of the form critics, are sermon material in two senses: they contain the church's remembrance of what Jesus said in his preaching and teaching, but this material comes to us in the form that it assumed in the preaching and teaching of the church and bears upon it the marks of its use in the church. Then, in much of the remainder of the New Testament, both in The Acts and in the Epistles, the apostolic ministry has, as its first responsibility, to preach the gospel. The ministry of Jesus Christ, with its prophetic anticipation and its apostolic continuation, is before all else the ministry of the word of God and as such a ministry of the spoken and written word.

It is necessary to emphasize this today because there are several quarters from which it is challenged. There is a widespread reaction in Protestantism against the prominence given to preaching, a reaction that is likely to grow much sharper if Protestant preaching in general continues in its present confusion of character. There is no Biblical or theological justification for the place we give to preaching in our services of worship if that preaching is nothing more than the random notes of the preacher on religion and life. Preaching that is the religious self-expression of the individual has no place anywhere in Christian worship. Preaching in which the personality of the preacher holds central place in the attention of the congregation is the height of blasphemy, for it is a man's egotistical insertion of himself at the point where God alone should stand. The only basis upon which the centrality of preaching can be justified and in which it is saved from being blasphemy is that it should be in the most thoroughgoing sense the ministry of God's word, in which the preacher takes upon himself so completely the form of a servant that he is forgotten and God himself in the power of his mighty truth makes himself known and commands all the attention of the congregation.

The second quarter in which the primacy of the preaching and teaching functions of the ministry is questioned is that part of the church which considers the priestly administration of the

Eucharist to be central. In the Roman Church the priestly act of daily repeating the sacrifice of Christ in the ceremony of the Mass takes precedence over all other duties, and preaching may occupy a very secondary place in the concerns and responsibilities of the priest. But also in some sections of the Protestant Church there is a similar though less extreme exaltation of the priestly and depression of the prophetic. One book may be cited as representing a viewpoint that is widely prevalent. In Norman Pittenger's *The Church, the Ministry, and Reunion* (1957), in spite of the conscious attempt of the author to avoid the excesses of an Anglo-Catholic viewpoint that leaves no way open for fellowship with Protestant churches, there is a complete ignoring of the whole prophetic tradition concerning the ministry in both Old and New Testaments. Because the Bible itself offers so little basis for a ministry that is primarily a priesthood, the Old Testament is ignored and the New Testament is interpreted as exhibiting only the undeveloped, incipient form of the ministry that was to reach its maturity and its definitive stage as a priesthood two hundred years later. Pittenger does not consider the possibility that these two centuries may have seen not only a legitimate development of Christian institutions but already the beginnings of a perversion of them that was to issue in the Roman order and in the subordination of the gospel to the institution.

To Reformed churchmen it is disturbing to find a remarkably similar viewpoint emerging in the book by T. E. Torrance that has already been mentioned. In faithfulness to his Reformed heritage and to the facts, this Scottish Presbyterian scholar gives due emphasis to the ministry of the word, but places it, in both Testaments, within the context of priesthood. It is the priest's and not the prophet's service of the word that he emphasizes, the prophets receiving very little attention. And so engrossed is he with the category of priesthood and sacrifice in his consideration of the ministry in the New Testament that he has practically nothing to say about the ministry of preaching and teaching in the activities of Jesus and of the apostles. It is true that in the Reformed churches there has been too little consideration of the

ministry as a priesthood and too little recognition of the centrality of the Eucharist alongside the word of preaching and
teaching. But the neglect is not likely to be corrected by a violent reaction in the opposite direction.

Emphasis upon priesthood always goes together with recognition of the importance of the sacramental element in the life
of the church. Not only in the Reformed churches but much
more widely throughout Protestantism there had been a neglect
of the sacraments and a loss of understanding of how essential
they are to the maintenance in the church of a true and living
communion with its Lord. We are ministers of the word and
sacraments and therefore priests as well as preachers and teachers.
The sacraments are a witness to the ultimate inadequacy of words
alone. We need to ask ourselves why the sacraments are necessary alongside the proclamation of the gospel. If we have set
Jesus Christ before the hearts and minds of men as adequately
as can be done in words, what more is needed? Here we are
confronted with the mystery of the gospel, which can never be
adequately expressed in words. The gospel that we try to state
in words is a person, and in that person it is God himself speaking to man and coming to man. All the words that Jesus spoke
to his disciples in his years with them were recognized by him
as insufficient to accomplish his purpose; it would be so easy
and natural for the disciples to turn his gospel into merely a
new religious doctrine and a new code of living. They would
be his church only in so far as the life that he possessed in himself in his oneness with God would continue to be their life,
binding them together into oneness with him and enabling him
to fulfill his redemptive purpose in them and through them.
Therefore, on the last night of his life he took bread and wine
and made them representations of his own being, that through
the years to come, as often as his disciples received the bread and
wine, they would be recalled to the living gospel and to the ministry that were incarnate in his own person. The sacrament is
thus a second, more direct, and simpler proclamation of the
gospel alongside the word, intended to guard the church through

all the ages from becoming the prisoner of its own words and ideas and from substituting a system of religious doctrines and practices for a personal Lord.

But if it is wrong to separate the sacraments from the preaching of the word, it is equally wrong to think that the sacraments can stand alone without the preaching of the word. There is a sacramentalism that regards the word and the sacraments as two separate channels of grace, the word of preaching being suitable only for one section of humanity who are specially equipped to respond to an intellectual presentation, and the Lord's Supper being a form of spiritual nourishment of universal appeal but particularly adapted to the needs of those who are less developed intellectually. Not only is this a false conception of preaching; it is also a transformation of the sacrament from its original unity with the ministry of the word into an independent sacred rite in which people are encouraged to think that they can enter into communion with Jesus Christ without taking the trouble to know him as he reveals himself in the record of the Scriptures. A sacramental mysticism is generated that can imperceptibly verge over into semipagan forms. The preaching of the word guards the sacrament from perversion just as the sacrament guards preaching from degenerating into a wooden transmission of right doctrines or ideas.

The Disappearance of Biblical Preaching

We have now to turn to some distressing implications of the statement that the centrality of preaching in the church can be justified only in so far as it continues the tradition of the prophets and apostles and dares to be a ministry of the word. Our distress is that preaching in the Protestant Church has in such large measure ceased to be an exposition of the word of God in Scripture. It is difficult to make generalizations about the kind of preaching that is being done in our varied denominations. We get a glimpse of what it is like at its best in published sermons. An examination of such volumes shows a profusion of topical sermons and a great scarcity of ones that wrestle in earnest with the meaning of Scripture for man's life. It is also significant that editors of religious publications have great difficulty in finding ministers with a sufficient grasp of Biblical interpretation to be able to write effectively on Biblical subjects. All the signs point to a widespread neglect of Biblical preaching, and, parallel with it, a colossal ignorance of the Bible among the laity. Topical preaching is the order of the day. A topic is developed that seems to be of interest to preacher and people alike, usually without any very close reference to Scripture, though a text may be used as a springboard at the beginning. Many ministers are convinced that this is the only kind of sermon to which modern American congregations will listen. Many of them also would admit that it is the only kind they can make interesting. Ministers of more than average competence and of unusual honesty have been known to confess that when they tried to break the habit of topical preaching and get back to serious Biblical preaching, each expository sermon they prepared was so dull and boring they could not bring themselves to preach it. In short, their own thoughts on religion and life were much more interesting and exciting to them than anything they could find in Scripture. That being true, they were well advised not to try Biblical preaching. But what kind of Bible is it that men find dull and boring? Perhaps there has first to be a rediscovery of the interest and excitement of the Bible before there can be any return to expository preaching.

One of the most critical situations confronting the Protestant church today is the disappearance of Biblical content from contemporary preaching. We know from our history books what happened in the medieval church when the Bible either fell into disuse or had its meaning concealed by a rank growth of allegorical interpretations. The church ceased to have in it any valid criterion by which to distinguish between true and false gospels or to discern what could or could not be done in the name of Jesus Christ. There is observable in the church today the same widespread failure in the power of discrimination. Any point of view that calls itself religious and is put forward with forcefulness and with attractive illustrations can secure a following, not just among ignorant people but even among some of the most highly educated. It is disturbing how few Christians can tell the difference between an attractively presented humanism and the Christian gospel. Even to many ministers it seems like quibbling to draw a sharp line between belief in the natural immortality of the soul and a Christian belief in death and resurrection. The idea is deeply rooted in the culture of our time that all religions are just variations upon a single theme, and the idea is rapidly spreading that while religion of some kind is very important as the foundation of our American civilization, its character need not be too sharply defined. We cannot see that "religion" may be man's chief defense against God. The ability to see any line of distinction between the Christian faith that has its origin in the person of Jesus Christ and forms of respectable religion both inside and outside the church that stop short of an unconditional relationship with God through Christ, has been lost widely in our churches, because that line of distinction can be seen today only when first it has been seen in the Scriptures. It runs between Amos and Amaziah, between Jeremiah and the religious reformers of his day, between Jesus and the most devoted and loyal exponents of Judaism, between Paul and many of his fellow Christians. Because we cease to see that line, we define the battle lines of the church as religion against irreligion, the church against secularism and materialism, or Christian civilization against unchristian civilization. That makes it simpler for us to be on the right side. But religion of a superior kind may be man's best bulwark against the radical claim upon him that God makes in Jesus Christ. When the Bible comes open in our midst, we are forced to see that God's battle line runs through the center of our American civilization, through the center of what we call religion, through the center of our churches, and through the center of our ministerial lives. The enemy we have to fight, the only enemy we need to fear, is within our own gates; it is the unbelief within ourselves that keeps us from being the church of Jesus Christ in truth and that remains hidden from us until the word of God in the Scriptures tears away all our self-deceptions and lays it bare before our eyes. In so far as we have let the Scriptures be silenced, we are a blind church at the mercy of our own unconscious self-deceptions and capable, like a blind church of nineteen hundred years ago, of betraying our Lord afresh. There is no safeguard against tragic self-betrayal for the church except an open Scripture from which Jesus Christ will speak the word that is a sharp, two-edged sword.

THE MAJOR SOURCES OF THE PROBLEM

We must ask the question now why there has been not just a decline but a disappearance of Biblical preaching. There are a number of factors that have contributed to this development. It is not to be construed as though the ministry of the church today were less responsible, less in earnest, or less consecrated than in some other day. Many of our most responsible, earnest, consecrated ministers find themselves unable to preach anything except topical sermons.

Perhaps the major force at work in the situation is to be located in the field of Biblical interpretation. The church has found itself suspended for some generations between two false alternatives in its approach to the Bible. On the one hand, there has been a historical, critical scholarship that has explored with the utmost thoroughness the literature, history, and religious phenomena of the Old and New Testaments but that either abandoned the category of revelation as being no longer useful in the description of Biblical religion, or, if it was retained, used it merely as a symbol of the higher moral and religious values of the literature. Intelligent, open-minded investigation of the Scriptures was thus combined with a denial of the central claim of the Scriptures to be the word of God. On the other hand, there has been constantly maintained in Protestantism an approach to Scripture that has insisted upon the reality of the revelation and its authority but that has refused to apply to the Bible the methods of literary and historical research that are accepted in the study of all other ancient literature. In this a valid protest against the blindness of historical, critical research to the revelation at the heart of the literature it was investigating was combined with a wholesale and undiscriminating rejection of the results of two hundred years of painstaking and devoted scholarship. On the one hand, we had a powerful witness to the humanity of the Bible and, on the other, a powerful witness to the divinity of God's word in the Bible, but we were placed in the false position of having to choose between these two. This is an oversimplification of the developments, but it does roughly describe the situation in which the church found itself. Fortunately, during the past twenty-five years this antithesis has begun to be overcome. The great achievement of Karl Barth in the 1920's was to force upon Biblical scholars the recognition that they had not taken the human witness of the Bible fully in earnest until they had given a hearing to the claim of the text to be a unique and decisive revelation of God. But he was not alone in seeing to the heart of the problem, and in the succeeding years Old and New Testament scholars have moved in varying degrees beyond merely literary, historical, and religious problems to the central reality of revelation. The hope that lies in this development is that there will be an ever-increasing flow of books that will provide us with an adequate introduction to the Scriptures both as a human record and as a divine revelation.

Our concern at the present moment, however, is with the effect of this false antithesis upon the use of the Bible in the church. Both approaches have contributed to the disappearance of Biblical preaching because both have left men unprepared to be inter-. preters of the text of Scripture. Perhaps one man's experience may be typical of many. In college and seminary we studied the languages, history, and literary problems of the Bible; we became familiar with it as a textbook of Hebrew and Christian religion. But when one day we found ourselves standing between the Scriptures and a congregation we were at a loss to understand how the words of this Book could become the very word of God to these people of the twentieth century. They were not interested in it as a textbook of ancient religions; they wanted bread to satisfy an urgent present hunger, and we were not ready to give it to them, at least not out of the Scriptures. Our training had not prepared us for that task. The easy way out of that dilemma was to prepare topical sermons and hang them on Biblical texts.

But the situation of the literalist whose training was the exact opposite was no different. He too, when he found himself standing between the Bible and a congregation, was at a loss. He was convinced that the Bible in all its parts was God's revelation, but when he tried to transfer that revelation directly to his people in preaching, something went wrong. There was a breakdown in communication and soon he found himself, in his earnest endeavor to make his preaching useful and meaningful to his people, forced into the groove of topical preaching. It is desperately hard to keep interest in the Bible alive if we close our eyes to all the marks of its humanity which bring it very close to us and enable us to find ourselves and our own human story in it.

A second factor in the situation has been the prevalence of an idea of revelation among religious people that excludes from consideration any claim of the Bible to be uniquely and exclusively the channel of revelation for Christians. Revelation is equated with truth in general, and God's revelation to man is taken to be merely another way of describing man's discovery through the ages of the truth concerning the world, himself, and God. Revelation is as broad as life itself. The beauty of nature, the loveliness of music, the riches of literature, are all revelations of God. We penetrate his mysteries in the records of history and we hear his voice in our own consciences. God speaks everywhere and in all things, and we have but to hear. And we as ministers are the exponents of this revelation of truth in general. How broad-minded that sounds! And in contrast how narrow-minded to suggest that the Christian revelation is accessible to us only between the two covers of the Bible! That has so often been scorned publicly as " shutting God up between the covers of a book." But is it any more narrow-minded than saying that God is never to be truly known except through one person, Jesus Christ? " No man cometh unto the Father, but by me." Is that narrowness or truth? God the Father remains the Lord of heaven and earth to whom all things belong and whose glory is manifest in every part of his creation. God is not made small by the assertion that at one point in the world's history, in the life and death and resurrection of Jesus of Nazareth, he has chosen to reveal himself in a way that he can be known nowhere else. Only in this narrow pass where we are confronted with God in Jesus Christ do we rightly learn who God is, and only through the Scriptures is it possible for us to come face to face with Jesus Christ. It is simply nonsense to say that *this* revelation is available in the beauties of nature, or the harmonies of music, or the profundities of great poetry. Whatever we find there (and it may be some of the choicest gifts of God), it is not for one moment to be confused with what finds us in the witness of the prophets and apostles and in Jesus Christ. Close the Scriptures and where in all the creation will man find any convincing witness that will lead him to believe in God the Father Almighty as his Heavenly Father, in Jesus Christ as his Lord and Savior, or in the Holy Spirit as the living Spirit of the Father and the Son dwelling in him and working through him today?

Consider, however, the effect of belief in a generalized revelation upon the life of the church. Let a man, whether he is minister or layman, really believe that he can know God merely by listening to the whispers of his own conscience or by reading poetry and history. Is he going to undertake the arduous task of working through the complex records of Scripture with their innumerable thorny problems in order to gain only a little more complete knowledge of God when for all practical purposes he seems to have an adequate knowledge from other sources? Twice (once in Canada and once in Switzerland), it has been my experience to have a preacher tell me that if I go out into my garden or into the mountains and open my heart to nature, I will learn all I need to know of God. If that is so, then have I not been a fool to waste years on the study of the Bible? And is not the minister who tries to make his people wrestle with the meaning of Scripture really troubling them unnecessarily? The aban-

donment of Scripture by the Protestant pulpit is a direct consequence of the loss of understanding in the church of the meaning
of the canon of Scripture, that strange line drawn in the first
and second centuries to mark off these writings from all other
writings as embodying an absolutely unique and exclusive revelation of God. The substitution of a generalized revelation, even
though the Scriptures are assigned a place of high honor and importance within it, brings inevitably a shift of focus and a de-
emphasizing of Scripture in the life of the church.

A third factor has been the persistent underestimation of the
difficulties of Biblical interpretation. The idea is widespread that
the Bible is a very simple book whose meaning should be evident,
without any great effort, to anyone who cares to read it, and certainly without any extensive background of knowledge. Actually
the Bible is a vast collection of ancient literature, composed by
a host of authors over a period of more than twelve hundred
years, in a world whose thought-forms were very different from
ours. There are close to a million words in it. The amazing thing
is that at so many points it speaks to us with such simplicity and
directness and makes us feel that it was written specifically for
us! And yet on every page it fairly bristles with problems and
difficulties of interpretation. It yields its meaning only to patient,
persistent study. It closes its doors to us when we become hurried
and impatient. And it is so easy for a modern pastor to become
hurried, with no time to wait before the word of Scripture for
its meaning to be revealed to him, no time for those careful
preparatory studies that are needed if we are to find our way to
the heart of Scripture in preaching and teaching.

A fourth factor, which is perhaps the most important of all, is
the existence in us, in our basic convictions, and in the structure
of the culture in which we live, of an approach to reality that is
fundamentally different from that which meet us in the Scriptures, and that, whether we are conscious of it or not, creates in
us a resistance to what they constantly try to say to us. We do not
want to hear the prophets or the apostles, and above all we do
not want to hear Jesus Christ (a resistance more likely subcon-

scious than conscious though none the less effective), because dimly we fear the revolution that might be required in us if we were ever brought into direct confrontation with the claim that God makes upon us through them. It is a great mistake to think that it is only the non-Christians whose beliefs and attitudes are in contradiction to the word of Scripture, and that when once we have become Christians the tension is resolved so that we can hear it without discomfort. No matter how earnestly Christian we are, we are webbed into a life in family, community, nation, and civilization in which countless forces are constantly at work drawing us in a direction contrary to that which, according to both Testaments, is the life-direction of the people of God. And within ourselves, no matter how truly in our baptism into Christ we have died unto self, the drive toward self-sovereignty persists, and unconsciously we seek to find tenable religious attitudes that will liberate us from complete and unconditional subjection to Jesus Christ. There is then inevitably a tension between the Scriptures and our entire human existence, even our most religious and most scrupulously moral existence, and it is not surprising that the human mind finds specifically religious devices for guarding its beloved structures against the cutting edge of the word of God.

The Roman Church, like rabbinical Judaism, has an authoritative tradition that shares the veneration in which Scripture is held and in which one can find refuge and support for established ideas and practices that would otherwise fare badly at the hands of the prophets. Protestant scholasticism, of which some forms still persist among us, developed a system of doctrine that it established as true by the proof-text method and then denied the possibility that anything in Scripture could ever contradict the system, thereby drawing a doctrinal screen over the Scriptures that prevented them from speaking their own word in freedom. Naïve souls in those days who read Scripture with their own eyes and not through the doctrinal screen and were so unwise as to say what they saw, might find themselves in serious trouble. Today one of the most widespread devices for silencing Scripture is the so-called " purely devotional approach," where it is domesticated to our familiar uses and made to serve our little needs by a careful elimination of the great central themes of Scripture that call us out of our engrossment with ourselves and claim us for the fulfillment of God's purpose for his world. But neither does the scholar escape from illusions. Historical, critical scholarship in the nineteenth and early twentieth centuries made the bold claim that it was teaching men to read Scripture without any vitiating presuppositions and so for the first time permitting the text to speak for itself. But today we are aware that critical scholars have always had their own theological assumptions and that what they have made of Scripture has been profoundly influenced by these assumptions. In spite of their scholarly techniques, they remain human beings who do not like to have their own most cherished convictions contradicted by Scripture. For instance, if they have no place in their theology for a revelation of a personal God to man, then the prophetic and apostolic claim to have received a revelation from God becomes for them an antiquated mythology that modern man must reinterpret in terms acceptable to our age.

There is perhaps no better illustration of this conflict between the mind that comes to expression in Scripture and our minds than the common conception of the " spark of divinity " in man. " Every man, however low he may sink, has in him a spark of the divine, so that it needs only to be blown upon to bring him alive and restore him to himself." To deny this spark seems to indicate a low view of man. Historically this idea of man had its origin in Greece and belongs in a theology in which God is the universal Mind, which permeates all things, creating order in them; and the mind of man is a fragment of this divine universal Mind. Man is therefore intrinsically divine, but not in his whole being, only in his mind. Not only is there no trace of this theology in Scripture; it is diametrically opposed to the conception of both God and man that we find there. In both Testaments God is a person who enters into relations with man, and man is a person created by God for fellowship with himself, but distinctly a mortal creature and never to be accounted divine. In

fact, his most acute temptation is his desire to cast off the limita-
tions and subordination of his creaturehood and be himself a
god. Also a "spark of divinity" is an impossible conception in
Scripture, for it implies an impersonal divine something rather
than a God who is never other than a person. The only way in
which there can be divinity in man according to Scripture is for
God in his Spirit to dwell in him, which means not a deifying
of the human ego but rather the reverse, the submission to God
of the human ego, with its consequent liberation (the service of
God, which is perfect freedom). But because it is sweeter to our
ears to hear that we are intrinsically divine and immortal, we
unconsciously evade the word of Scripture that would strip us
of our pleasant illusions about ourselves. And the preacher who
feels called to preach the gospel of the divine spark in man is
not likely to feel any compulsion to deal faithfully with Scripture.

THE PROPHETIC AND APOSTOLIC GOSPEL

Already some features of the case for expository preaching have
been suggested, but we need to gather them together in a more
definite and systematic fashion. By expository preaching is not
meant some one form of Biblical exposition but rather any form
of preaching that attempts seriously to get at the content of the
Biblical text and to let it become meaningful in the contemporary
situation. Therefore, when we say that expository preaching is
the only legitimate form of Christian preaching, we are merely
insisting that preaching have its source in and draw its content
from the gospel that is available to us only through the medium
of the Scriptures. So stated, the principle seems beyond dispute if
Christian preaching is to be the preaching of the Christian gospel,
and yet it is so widely disregarded that, if the church were to
take it with the same seriousness that it did in the days of the
Reformation, there would be nothing less than a revolution in the
character of the church's preaching.

The content of the gospel is a person, Jesus Christ, and not a
series of Biblical doctrines or a set of principles illustrated by
Biblical stories. In him the gospel is "event in history." The

Word of God takes human form in him, in his life and teaching, his death and resurrection, and is known to us as the Word in which all the meanings of our life in its height and depth and length and breadth are revealed to us. In him, God comes into our human life to redeem it, and all things in our life are lifted up where they can be seen and known in their true light in relation to God. But this person, Jesus Christ, is not known to us as an isolated individual; he is known to us only in the context of the prophets and the apostles. He can no more be torn apart from them than a bird can be torn out of the context of its wings and still remain a bird. The apostolic context is the easier of the two to establish. A generation ago the aim of many scholars was to isolate the historic Jesus from the apostles so that we might see him directly and no longer through their eyes. The Synoptic Gospels were thought to offer the opportunity for escape from what was termed " apostolic distortions." But more careful study of the Synoptic Gospels in recent years has established the fact that they too are apostolic witness and embody in them a very considerable measure of apostolic interpretation. We see Jesus through the eyes of the apostles or we do not see him at all. Jesus and his apostles have been welded into a unity so intimate that any attempt to cut the two apart results in a mutilation of both. A distinction between them may and must be seen but never in such a way as to conceal the unity of the gospel in them.

It is the second context that even some of our ablest scholars and theologians are inclined to ignore, Jesus' context in the Old Testament. Few New Testament scholars take Jesus' relation to the Old Testament seriously; many ignore it almost completely. They interpret the New Testament in the context of Judaism and Hellenism but not in the context of the Old Testament. And yet Jesus can no more be isolated from the prophets than from the apostles without being completely misrepresented. To divorce him from the Old Testament is to tear him and his ministry and his gospel out of the organic historical and theological relationship in which they belong. Until we recognize how completely one with the prophets Jesus was, we cannot see how or where he goes beyond the prophets and is the fulfillment of the work of God begun in them. The very existence of Jesus is rooted in the Old Testament, not the Old Testament as understood by the rabbis, but the Old Testament as Jesus, in fulfilling its meaning and purpose, understood it and reinterpreted it. The baptism and temptation stories, interpreted not as constructs of the church but as valid witness to experiences of Jesus, make plain to us that God spoke to Jesus through the medium of the Old Testament. The word of God, which is the bread of life to him, is not a totally new word in radical discontinuity from all that has been known before but is acknowledged by him to be in direct continuity with the word of God in the Old Testament. It was no accident, then, that the New Testament church made the Old Testament Scriptures its own. As C. H. Dodd brings out so effectively in his book *According to the Scriptures,* it was not only the New Testament church but it was Jesus himself who saw the pattern of his gospel in the Old Testament and used it from the beginning as a primary witness to the truth that was incarnate in his own being. To be ministers of Jesus Christ, therefore, is to be concerned with the entire witness to him in both Testaments.

Expository preaching is thus all preaching that opens the Scriptures and finds in them that word of God to man which has its focus in the person of Jesus Christ. There are some forms of preaching that make a pretense of being Biblical but actually evade the essential task. The retelling of a Bible story is not necessarily Biblical preaching, and, if it serves only to support a platitudinous moral, as it often does, it is the direct antithesis of Biblical preaching. One thing the Bible never does is to moralize, and the preacher who gives his people the impression that it is a book of religious stories, each with a very simple moral, has utterly perverted the character of the Bible. Nor is a sermon Biblical that confines itself exclusively to the discussion of a passage of Scripture. It is the nature of Scripture that it is focused always on life, not on abstract religious truths but on concrete historical life situations. The word of God is a word addressed to specific human beings in the dilemmas and complications of their existence. Therefore, preaching that goes round and round inside the text of Scripture and is filled to the brim with Biblical material but never comes into focus upon the actualities of the lives of those who are being addressed is most unbiblical in its character.

Anyone who is familiar with Calvin's sermons may think of expository preaching as a series of running comments on the verses of a passage, drawing out its theological content and relating it to life. One marvels at the vitality of many of Calvin's sermons after four hundred years. And only those who are ignorant of the magnitude of his achievement as a Biblical interpreter and preacher could speak of him with other than respect. (See T. H. L. Parker, *The Oracles of God,* Lutterworth Press, 1947, an excellent presentation and discussion of Calvin's preaching.) But surely it is no word of disrespect to suggest that a method effective in Geneva in the sixteenth century may be most ineffective today. In fact, there is reason to believe that the use of this method in a later time did much to bring expository preaching into disrepute. It can easily degenerate into a succession of comments on a chapter of Scripture that can be very dull. It is a method that can tempt a busy minister into lazy and careless preparation for preaching. The revival of such a method would not be likely to help toward a rebirth of effective Biblical preaching. A sermon must have unity and structure.

There is a wide variety of forms that Biblical preaching may take. A lengthy text is not a necessity, for the message of Scripture may come to utterance in a very brief text. It is not quantity of Scripture that is important. Many texts, however, demand for their right understanding that they be heard in their larger context. The sermon may be the exposition of an incident or it may wrestle with the significance of a single character, but always asking what place that incident or character has in the total Biblical revelation. Again it may deal with a doctrine, not developing the doctrine in logical abstraction but rather seeing it in its organic relationship within the Biblical understanding of God's dealings with man. It would be useful in educating people to read the Scriptures for themselves if there were more often series of sermons on single books. There is also a place for a sermon that introduces people at one sitting to a whole book of the Bible. But in all these instances the principle holds true that it is Biblical preaching only when through the sermon the Bible is permitted to speak its own unique message to the man of today. A purely informational sermon as an introduction to understanding Scripture is never a wise procedure. It is as unwise as a purely informational sermon about Jesus Christ would be.

In conclusion, let us ask what is the long-range effect, on the one hand, of topical preaching, and, on the other, of expository preaching. Topical preaching is by its very nature ephemeral. It seizes upon the topic of the moment and for that very reason may have an initial interest and impact far greater than most expository sermons. But because it relates itself *primarily* to the passing events of time, it passes from the mind with the swiftness of time itself. Moreover, since its point of origin is to be traced no farther back than the person of the preacher, and its authority and impressiveness are the authority and impressiveness of his understanding of God and man and life, it tends to make the congregation dependent upon the preacher. He is the source of their spiritual inspiration and understanding. Take him away and they are bereft. But expository preaching by its nature constantly points the congregation beyond the preacher to the Source of light and life as he makes himself known in the Scriptures. Every genuine Biblical sermon has the effect of opening the Scriptures one stage wider for the congregation so that step by step they are being equipped to live out of the infinite resources that are available to them in the Scriptures. Expository preaching thus creates a church in which the people no longer are centered upon the preacher in the same measure but have their faith grounded in the revelation of the Scriptures, so that their life as a Christian congregation has in it a stability that is not possible in any preacher-centered church. The ultimate hope of expository preaching is that a congregation should so come under the power of the Word and Spirit of God that it would be remolded into a ministering fellowship in which every member would know himself called to be a servant of the Word.

4

THE TEACHING MINISTRY

ELSEWHERE I have written at greater length on the teaching ministry of the church and I must avoid a mere repetition of what I have said there. In the present context the educational task must be seen from the standpoint of how it enters into the fulfillment of the total ministry. Paul, in Eph. ch. 4, sets the unity of the ministry in line with an impressive sequence of other unities — one body, one Spirit, one hope, one Lord, one faith, one baptism, one God and Father of us all, and one ministry in which apostles, prophets, evangelists, pastors, and teachers are all joined and knit together. It is evident that Paul was concerned with something much deeper than a superficial or sentimental oneness in which people merely maintain a kindly disposition toward one another as they go their separate ways. The ministry for him was an organic unity in which each part was essential to all the other parts. The possession of one ministry by Christians was like their possession of one God, one Spirit, one hope, one faith. The apostle might hold a very distinguished position in the church, and the teacher in some local congregation might think his status in the ministry to be very lowly and obscure, but each, says Paul, is essential to the total ministry, and weakness at either point is disastrous for the whole. But the unity reaches even farther. The apostle in order to discharge fully his responsibility as an apostle has to share in the work of the teacher, and the teacher whose task it is to instruct a group of young converts has to let his mind and heart and soul be filled with the same faith and knowledge of which the apostle is so decisively a living witness. Only in oneness with the apostle in faith can the teacher fulfill his ministry.

We must confess frankly that in the contemporary church we sin deeply against this principle of the unity of the ministry. We have permitted various forces to split the ministry into fragments, each aspect of it claiming to be a whole ministry and able to pursue its task in relative isolation from other forms of ministry. The theological seminary is acutely aware of this fragmentation in the theological disciplines and of how difficult it is to keep the curriculum from proceeding as though each aspect of ministry could be developed within the student in isolation from all other aspects, the student himself being left to find some unity in his fragmented training if he can. The forms of disunity with which we are here concerned, however, are not so much those within the structure of theology itself as those between the scientific theologian and the preacher-pastor-teacher and between the preacher-pastor and the teacher in the local church.

The gap between the Biblical-theological scholar and the pastor or teacher in the local church is wide; not so wide as it was earlier in this century, yet still distressingly so. This is in part due to the abdication by pastors and teachers of their theological responsibility (see Chapter 6), many of them early in their ministries ceasing to be students seeking out through the medium of books those who are able to guide them ever farther in their Christian development. They think themselves able to fulfill their ministries without this fellowship in learning. But responsibility for the gap must also be placed upon the Biblical and theological scholar who has been so concerned to establish the scientific character of his specialty that he has largely forgotten that his entire work belongs within the full, rich context of the ministry of Jesus Christ and of the church of Jesus Christ. The distinguished president of a society of Biblical scholars recently in his presidential address emphasized over and over that the Biblical scholar is a scientific philologist and historian and not a theologian. Though himself a devoted churchman, he felt it necessary, in order to safeguard the scientific integrity of Biblical research, to isolate the Biblical from all other departments of theological investigation. He seemed to be unaware that he was really saying that the Biblical scholar, in so far as he is scientific in his work, is isolated from the ministry of Jesus Christ and from the theological responsibility that rests upon that ministry in every part. There is also a hidden assumption in this point of view that the more firmly and coherently one believes the Christian faith, the less honest he is likely to be in his examination and interpretation of the phenomena that meet him in the Scriptures. Biblical scholarship that proceeds from this standpoint is likely to lose its pertinence for the life of the church and its interest for the preacher and teacher. A comparison of the commentaries of Luther and Calvin with many of our modern commentaries is illuminating in this respect. In scientific knowledge of history and literary analysis, as one would expect, the Reformers are hopelessly antiquated. Many of their theological interpretations of particular texts are no longer tenable. But there is in them frequently a theological penetration that is missing in many modern commentaries, and on every page one is made aware that it is a minister of the church of Jesus Christ in the fullest sense who is interpreting for us the significance of the words of the Scriptures. The Biblical exegete is also theologian, preacher of the gospel, teacher of the church, and pastor of the flock. The Reformers claim their full ministry while still discharging in the most responsible way their special ministry in exegesis. Can there be any doubt that if the modern scholar were in like manner to claim his full ministry, his commentaries would be, not less scientific, but much more edifying to preachers, teachers, and laymen in the church?

The gap between preacher-pastor and educator varies in depth among different denominations, but there can be few who do not have some experience of it. Many educators have had bitter experience of it. They chose in their student days to spend their lives in the educational work of the church. This was their vocation. They received a training in preparation for it as thorough as that of any preacher or pastor. They minister to all ages of children, young people, and adults, only occasionally preaching from the pulpit but continually in a hundred other ways confronting persons with the meaning of the Christian gospel. They have frequently to do the work of a pastor in counseling those who are under their care. But rarely are they regarded as being in the ministry; they are in something that, while it is recognized as an essential Christian service and vocation, is not quite the ministry. In some denominations they are not called " ministers," or ordained as ministers, or permitted to sit in the policy-making courts of the church as ministers of the church. Most painful of all is the unspoken assumption (which, however, makes itself evident in numerous practical arrangements) that the preacher or pastor belongs on a different level from the educator in the life of the church. It has not been unknown in the past for a highly trained educator to be sent on office-boy errands for the much more important pastor. This distinction of levels cannot be dismissed as a phenomenon that is found only in unenlightened and retrograde regions; it is encouraged and perpetuated in most of our seminaries by the double standard of curriculum — for preachers and pastors on the one hand and for educators on the other. Even in our best seminaries it is assumed that a person who is to direct an educational program does not need the same thorough training in Bible, church history, and systematic theology that is considered necessary for preachers and pastors. Yet as a rule the educator in the local church has far more to do with Bible teaching, the interpretation of church history to children and adults, and the discussion of theological problems with all ages of people than has the pastor. There are seminaries where the disparity of standards between the two departments is so great that the Biblical and theological textbooks used for religious education students would not be recognized as adequate in the theological department. There is no hope for the overcoming of the double standard until there is rebellion among educators themselves against such obvious and unreasonable concessions to it.

The distinction between the two was greatly sharpened by the tendency in the first half of this century for religious education, in its zeal for educational thoroughness, to follow a line of develment that was separating it ever more widely not only from other theological disciplines but also from the historical continuity of the church's life. Religion and ethics in their broadest sense (so broad as to become almost identical in some instances with the democratic community) became the context of religious education, rather than the apostolic faith with its intransigent center in Jesus Christ. Where this happened, the gap became so wide that it was difficult for the opposing sides even to conduct a conversation with each other. This most certainly helped to consolidate the double standard, but as it becomes ancient history and religious education rediscovers its place in the theological disciplines, its roots in the Christian faith, and its context in the church, it becomes more possible for preacher, pastor, and educator to acknowledge their sharing together one ministry.

PREACHERS AND PASTORS BUT NOT EDUCATORS

It is one of the by-products of this divorce and double standard that so many ministers do not regard teaching as an essential part of their ministry. Jesus was a teacher. Paul was a teacher. But these ministers are not teachers! They are preachers and pastors, which they somehow take for granted to be a calling more important, and perhaps more distinguished. Because of this blind spot in regard to the teaching aspect of their task, they fail to equip themselves in seminary for the work of teaching. One has only to think of the monstrously inappropriate stories that preachers who tell children's stories in the service of worship will inflict upon small children. A famous one began: "Now you children will all have seen in the newspapers about the man with a case of amnesia who was picked up last week on the streets of our city"—a prelude to the story of the prodigal son. An equally famous one, for four- and five-year-olds, explained to them the Latin derivation of the word "sincere"—*sine cera*, without wax. Even an elementary course on the psychological development of childhood would have prevented such absurdities. But apparently neither of the guilty parties had felt he needed any educational training in order to fulfill his ministry. The minister who is not equipped to teach is like a soldier who is trained to meet only half the situations and opportunities that are likely to arise in the course of the battle and who congratulates himself that he has the training to meet the more important situations and opportunities. He stands a fair chance of losing the battle.

It may be of value for one minister to review the history of his own ministry in relation to teaching. In seminary the educational aspect of the ministry was totally ignored. I do not remember its ever being mentioned that the church school had any place in the pastor's responsibility. In the British tradition of emphasizing Biblical studies, systematic and historical theology, and the history and philosophy of religion, and of de-emphasizing the practical, our curriculum made only slight provision even for homiletics and pastoral theology. This does not mean, however, that there was no interest whatever in educational problems in general, but it remained general rather than specific and did not focus upon the peculiar problems that confront the church in education.

In my first pastorate the conditions in the church school were deplorable, the superintendent being a deeply earnest Christian man who had no understanding of education and who equated the Christian faith with the most rigid type of legalistic literalism. The curriculum materials were not those of the denomination but were imported in order to secure in them a literalism that would correspond with the convictions of the superintendent. Several of the teachers were persons of real competence who did excellent work in spite of the circumstances. I myself did what I could in an auxiliary capacity. But it never occurred to me to take steps to secure a totally different order in the church school. It was an independent organization within the congregation, similar to a women's missionary society, with lay leadership, and it was unthinkable that I as minister should interfere in any radical way in either of them. The church school was not my responsibility in the same way that preaching and pastoral work were. I had my own opportunity to teach in an adult group on Wednesday evenings, and I had to be satisfied with that, hoping that eventually my teaching would undermine the established order in the church school and secure a change. I was called to another parish before that change was effected.

In my next pastorate, a much larger congregation, there was no problem with literalism or literalistic curriculum materials, but there were acute problems with the church school. The superintendent himself had a very limited education, both in general and in the Christian faith, and had little understanding of what is involved in religious education. He had been thrust into the position by the session of the congregation as the only one among them who was willing to take time for it, and he could not have been more loyal or efficient in administering the school. He kept its wheels turning in the identical way in which they had been turning for years. He managed somehow to occupy the twenty-five-minute period of " opening exercises " that in his experience had always been occupied by the superintendent. He maintained a staff of teachers, though at least half of them had little interest in teaching and would not use any opportunities offered for improving their knowledge and competence. Class time, brief as it was, was rudely interrupted by pupils being called out of the room to repeat verses of Scripture that they were memorizing in a general program of memorization that the school had had in operation for some years. It produced a nice, visible array of awards at the end of the year and gave everyone a satisfying feeling of something concrete accomplished. But education was not being taken seriously. I acted as supply teacher for a time in order to secure a fairly wide contact with the pupils and was made aware of how little most of them were learning about the Christian faith. I organized a teacher-training class to which only the more competent teachers came, never more than one quarter of the teaching staff. Finally I took on the teaching of a youth class before church on Sunday morning in an attempt to reach the pupils in some more thorough way before they passed beyond the church school. But again it did not occur to me that the ineffective order of the church school was my responsibility and that I should not permit it to continue any more than I would myself continue with some plainly wasteful and hopeless method of preparing sermons. Education was an area of the church's life in which I might participate because of my interest and concern, but it was not a primary responsibility of my ministry. In the last resort what happened in the church school was the responsibility of laymen.

In my last year in this parish something happened that was to have far-reaching consequences for me. The congregation was growing in a satisfactory manner. There was evidences of progress at various points. I liked my people. My work seemed to be going well. But suddenly I became conscious of what can only be described as a sense of spiritual suffocation, an awareness of something seriously wrong. As the distress continued I was forced to probe to the bottom of it. I made a careful re-examination of the structure of my ministry. I discovered that I was spending 95 per cent of my time with people over thirty years of age. I knew all the adults in my congregation intimately, but I did not know the children and young people intimately. It is true that it is much harder to make contact with them than with the adults, but I could not claim to have tried too hard. In a congregation of over nine hundred members, when one has no assistance of any kind, it is very easy for most of a minister's time to be preoccupied with adult concerns. And yet it is the adult after the age of thirty who is likely to be most difficult to change from his established patterns of thinking and acting. It became clear that I had been expending most of my energies at the point where they were least likely to produce results and only a tiny fraction of my time at the point where the lives of my people were most open to be molded and refashioned by the Christian gospel. In the light of this discovery I began a reconstruction of my ministry, and as

I focused it more directly upon the younger members of the community, I found myself more intimately involved in educational situations and the sense of suffocation began to vanish.

In my third parish, a still larger one, the situation was very similar to the one just described, except that the opening exercises were longer and the class period shorter. The superintendent was better educated and more competent, but he too was the prisoner of a system. He felt it his duty to carry forward the church school in much the same order in which it had been entrusted to him. The brevity of the class periods made it difficult to enlist the services of anyone who would be really interested in teaching. With the resignation of the superintendent I did the unheard-of thing of taking over the position myself in order to have freedom for experiment and change and with the hope of training someone to provide a new kind of leadership. I gave priority in pastoral visitation to the homes of children in the church school, announcing to the congregation that I was doing so. At last I had found the balanced unity of my ministry, with education taking its place alongside preaching and pastoral responsibilities and closely interwoven with them. It was not just one more responsibility added; it was a restructuring of the entire ministry with extremely important implications both for the character of preaching and the character of pastoral work.

MEMBERS OF AN AUDIENCE OR ORGANIZATION BUT NOT DISCIPLES

The question that naturally poses itself for consideration at this point is, What difference does it make in the total character of the ministry when it fails to be a teaching ministry? An allied question is, What consequences does it have for the total character of the church? Perhaps the way in which to pose the question is, What if Jesus had contented himself with the proclamation of the gospel of the Kingdom and had not taken time for teaching? He would have had converts and those converts would somehow or other have become organized into religious societies, but he would not have had disciples, at any rate not disciples with sufficient understanding of his gospel to share with him in the proclamation of it. That is why teaching is essential to the ministry of Jesus. In his teaching he was training his converts to participate with him in the liberation of humanity into its true existence in the Kingdom of God, that is, into a life in which all things and all experiences have their significance transformed by a transition of man from isolation and alienation into a oneness with God that makes possible a new openness in his relations with his fellow men. The oneness with God was not a mystical identification with God but a personal I-Thou relation in which God was sovereign and man was servant, with the sovereignty not of an arbitrary tyrant but like that of a father, and with a servanthood not slavish but like that of a son. Jesus was not interested merely in having a succession of audiences to which either he, or someone on his behalf, might proclaim his gospel; he was interested primarily in having disciples in whom and through whom his ministry would be multiplied many times over. Therefore, his proclamation of the gospel, which brought men to repentance and made them willing to commit themselves to God in faith, had to be followed by teaching in which he came into a more intimate relation with the converts and began a process of training that had as its ultimate goal their participation in his mission. The elimination of his teaching would therefore constitute a change that would affect the total character of his ministry and his church.

When we turn from the Gospel to the situation of the present day, we are met by the fact that congregations are to such a great degree audiences that come together once each week for a period of worship and for the hearing of a sermon rather than communities of Christian disciples in training for the fulfillment of a ministry. This is the direct consequence, the result that should be expected, from a ministry that abdicates its teaching responsibility. The preaching of the gospel merely brings men to the threshold of discipleship. If they are to cross the threshold and become, in the true sense, disciples, that is, learners or students, they must have a teacher. The two terms are correlative, disciple and teacher, and where there is no teacher but only a preacher, one need not expect to find disciples.

Here we touch one of the most acute problems of our American Christianity — that such a high percentage of those who call themselves Christians are members of an audience or of an organization and not disciples, not students of the faith in training for some kind of definite service. But before we criticize them too severely for this, we should recognize that they are the direct product of a ministry that concentrates on preaching and organizing and leaves teaching to someone else. And most likely the preaching they have heard has not even made them aware that a Christian needs not only to hear the gospel and respond in faith and obedience but also to embark upon a course of study through which alone he can find his true growth in faith and knowledge and power for action. It is clear, then, that preaching which is divorced from teaching misrepresents the claim that Jesus Christ makes upon the person who responds to him and who desires to enter into fellowship with him. It says, " Become a regular member of this audience, take regularly of the sacrament of the Lord's Supper, and let your daily life be such as befits one who follows Christ, and you will be in full communion with Jesus Christ and his church." But in the Gospels, Jesus says that to be in communion with him is to be a disciple, abiding in his word and with his word of truth abiding in us, liberating us from our ignorance and blindness and from all that incapacitates us for his service. How can there be communion with Jesus Christ if there is no thought, no intention, of entering upon a life of discipleship?

The weakness of the church at many crucial points arises directly from this failure of members of the church to become disciples of Jesus Christ. It causes a tragic shortage of competent lay leaders because so few mature adults have any thorough education in the faith to which they are earnestly committed. Their Christian education ceased in their teens. They have read little or nothing about their faith. (Although the sale of religious novels and religious books that are like spiritual get-rich-quick manuals is sometimes large, books that would be useful for growth in real discipleship have a pitifully small sale in a nation where there are supposed to be one hundred and ten million Christian disciples.) They have nothing more than the education they have received in Sunday morning worship. The consequence often is that men become lay leaders in the church not because of any unusual development or competence or understanding of a peculiarly Christian nature but because of their eminence in their business or profession or because of their engaging personal qualities. They have the character of a leader but not the knowledge or understanding or penetrating Christian judgement that are necessary to empower them for Christian leadership.

An equally serious consequence is the perennial shortage of teachers for the church school and the incapacity of parents to give intelligent guidance and help to their own children in their growth in faith. It is futile to expect a person to teach others who is not engaged in a process of learning himself. The whole thing must then be routine and mechanical, and consequently boring for both teacher and pupils. Only the person who in his own study of the Christian faith is aware that he is engaged in a venture not just in understanding but in " being," which is more important and exciting than anything else in life, should be permitted to teach others. The nondisciple, when by some device he is cornered and persuaded to take on a class in church school, is likely to expend only a bare minimum of time in preparation, grudging even that minimum, to take no interest in the class beyond the brief period that he is compelled to spend with them, and to escape from the responsibility at the earliest possible moment. Some church schools have as much as 50 per cent turnover in teaching staff each year, an indication that they are heavily loaded with nondisciples.

Perhaps the place where the consequences are most tragic of all is where the church meets the world. This in itself is a very large subject, for it includes not just the contact of the church with the world of unbelief outside its doors but also the manifold meetings of church and culture, church and community, church and state. We must first recognize that rarely does the church meet the world with a trained minister or theologian present to speak for the church. We may from time to time arrange such meetings in which we try to provide competent representation for the church. But each day countless unarranged meetings of church and world are taking place as members of the church go about their normal business in the world, and they have no escape from being the representatives of the church before the world with the cause of Christ resting upon their shoulders.

There is constantly the meeting of faith with unbelief. It is in the incidental contacts of life that man in the agony or in the exuberance of his unbelief unveils himself to what he takes to be a representative of the community of faith. He may be aggressively mocking or condescendingly scornful or pathetically helpless or bitter with hostility, but in each instance he is at least exposing himself to the possibility of an answer, one never knows from what depth of despair. In that situation the Christian dare not say, "If only I could get you to come to church." As a Christian he himself *is* the church, the only church there is in that situation, and if he has nothing to answer, the church goes down to defeat before the world in its unbelief. The battle front between belief and unbelief is manned by laymen, not by seminary-trained ministers. The minister's task is to train the laymen to give a good account of themselves in the battle, and from time to time he himself has the opportunity of making immediate contact with the other side; but on the whole he is compelled by his duties to spend most of his time behind the lines, and the church has to rely upon its rank and file for the steady day-by-day contest. And we ought to know that the fate of communities, nations, and whole civilizations depends upon the outcome of that contest. What chance has the church of Jesus Christ if its front-line soldiers are untrained, vague, and confused in their understanding of the Christian faith and unable to speak coherently on its behalf?

There is also the meeting of church and culture. The character of the culture in which we live molds our lives imperceptibly from earliest years. The school is the chief agent of culture but only the chief among a multitude of forces, and with the advent of television its primacy is challenged by a powerful rival. Newspapers, books, magazines, picture shows, art, architecture, music,

the theater, modern forms of folklore, the mechanical appurte-
nances of our life, all participate in establishing the patterns of our
culture, but the way in which they are built together and the
meaning they have for us is determined by the faith that is the
organizing principle in society. In any culture there is bound to
be a conflict of faiths and therefore a conflict of organizing principles. Some cultural forms may assume a character that is irre-
concilable with the Christian faith, so that the Christian whose
life is being shaped by them finds his culture to be in insufferable tension with his faith. Education may be captured by a
philosophy of life, a conception of man and of the goals of human
life, that a Christian must repudiate or cease to be a Christian.
But again, an education that claims to be Christian and that has
a simple solution to every cultural problem may, in its naïveté,
be simply bad education in the context of formal Christian doctrine and so equally a threat to the existence of the Christian.
Some churches in past and present have thought to escape the
cultural problem by cutting the community of believers apart
from the outside world that they may live only in a world that
is consonant with their faith. But there is no escape. They merely
create a new and different culture of their own that suffers from
its own peculiar corruptions, and they soon find that the cultural
realm outside has its ways of seeping into their enclosed world.
The cultural question is therefore inescapable and urgent for the
church; in fact, if it takes seriously the claim of the risen Christ
that the whole of man's life belongs to him, it can no longer desire
to escape from the dilemma but on the contrary discovers in
every aspect of culture God's good gifts, which are to be received
with thanksgiving and with the confidence that these too are intended to serve God's glory. But how shall the Christian see distinctions in his culture if he has not gone much beyond the ABC's
in his exploration of the Christian faith?

The same is true in the Christian's relation to the state. He is at
one and the same time a responsible member of the church, who
has vowed to render obedience to Jesus Christ as his only absolute Lord, and a responsible citizen of the state, bound to obey

the lawful government of the nation and to be loyal at all times. It is superficial folly to think that a line can be drawn between church and state, so that there is no conflict between the two loyalties, or that a man may keep his citizenship and his Christianity in separate compartments. Jesus Christ claims a total loyalty of his followers, that they should bring all things in their individual, social, economic, and political life into obedience to him. And the state, particularly in its modern semitotalitarian forms, is constantly reaching beyond the external regulation of things necessary for ordered life in the community to the control of men's thoughts and attitudes. Even though the state itself may not attempt to control the souls of men, self-appointed representatives and spokesmen for the national interest may not be so restrained and may use vicious propaganda and intolerable social pressures to coerce the souls of men into the acceptance of some brand of nationalism. What hope has the church to stand against such a threat as this unless the rank-and-file Christian is sufficient of a disciple to recognize the peril of his situation and to persist in a citizenship that is the more profoundly loyal to his nation the more he refuses to compromise in his loyalty to Jesus Christ? The church member who has not thought sufficiently about the nature of his faith even to be aware of the possibility of a conflict between his loyalty to Christ and his loyalty to the state is not likely to give a good account of himself when he suddenly finds himself in the midst of an inflamed nationalism.

The situation of our day, then, calls for a church of disciples, and only too often it calls in vain. A preaching and pastoral and priestly ministry may build large congregations and impressive organizations, but only when there is added to them an effective teaching ministry does the church begin to become a fellowship of disciples.

EDUCATORS AND NOT PREACHERS OR PASTORS

The divorce between the various aspects of ministry may, however, have quite different consequences when it is the teaching ministry that proceeds in independence and is cut apart from its total context in the whole ministry of Jesus Christ. If there have been preachers and pastors who have said, "We are not called to teach," there have been educators who have said, "We are not called to do anything other than teach." Teaching appeals to some persons as a more practical and down-to-earth occupation than preaching. The situation seems to be more under control. The psychology of child development enables one to measure with reasonable accuracy where the pupils are in their growth and to adapt the teaching to their specific present needs. There are ways of determining their strengths and weaknesses of character and of planning a curriculum and program of activities that will remedy the weaknesses and shape the character in the desired direction. By tests we can ascertain what they know about the Bible or about the Christian faith in general, and direct our attention to their points of ignorance and confusion. We can by careful preparation arrange periods of worship for them that will provide them with the religious experiences that are essential to their healthy spiritual development. In short, whereas the preaching situation is vague and uncontrolled, so that the preacher is making a stab in the dark, hoping his words may apply to someone, the teaching situation is a controlled one in which by the use of the right techniques we can determine with reasonable accuracy the outcome. Education has in the modern age become a science, the science of human development, that may indeed in the secular sphere be used by humanists to work toward humanist goals, but that the Christian educator is able to adapt without too much difficulty to Christian purposes. The fishing pole that the poacher uses for a criminal purpose becomes a Christian fishing pole, when, in the hands of a Christian, it is used to catch fish in a law-abiding way!

It is at this point that the Christian educator needs to be reminded that he is a minister of Jesus Christ, and that he will do well to consider why Jesus was both preacher and teacher, and that, when Jesus turned to the task of teaching, he did not cease to be the proclaimer of the gospel. In the making of disciples even Jesus did not have the process under control. It was a work of the

Spirit of God, which he served with his whole being, with his preaching and with his teaching, but the Spirit was not subject to his direction. "The wind blows where it wills." (John 3:8.) Even Jesus followed only where the Spirit led. He preached his gospel, but he did not know where among his hearers the seed would find its way into good, deep soil and the Spirit of God at work in the seed of the word would claim another life for the Kingdom. Who would respond to the call of the gospel was a mystery that no eye could pierce and no science determine.

This inability of Jesus to communicate directly to men the truth of God is nowhere more evident than in the revelation to the disciples of his Messiahship. The whole Christian movement was eventually to have as its dynamic center the conviction that Jesus was Christ and Lord. Some scholars question whether Jesus believed this of himself. But if he did (and there are excellent reasons for holding that he did), this was a knowledge that he could not convey in words even to his most intimate disciples, for his Messiahship was the mystery of who he was in relation to God. Therefore, he had to wait for the mystery to be revealed to them when they were ready for the revelation, and with the possibility that they might never be ready for it. Judas stands for all time as a stubborn witness to the fact that Jesus was not able to control the outcome of the education of his disciples. Where there was an inner resistance to the Spirit of God his words succeeded only in creating a superficial likeness of a disciple, not a real disciple. We ought not to forget that Judas responded sufficiently to give up his normal occupation and to become a member of the Twelve and that he was trained for the ministry, but there was a decision in his relation to God that Judas never made and an ultimate response that he never gave.

It is this mystery in the making of a Christian that the religious educator is inclined to forget. He begins to think that he has a technique by which the desired result can be secured. He can do it by education. But if the desired result is really the making of a Christian, that is, a person in whom self has been dethroned and God in his Spirit is sovereign, and who, because of his unconditional openness to God, is unconditionally open to his fellow man, the claim is that education can control and produce a development in human beings that, according to the New Testament, is the work of the Holy Spirit through the gospel of Jesus Christ. But to claim to do what only God can do is blasphemy!

The teacher of theology is in a like danger of falling into blasphemy if he speaks as though the knowledge of God were something that can be directly communicated to students. God in the Old Testament, God in the New Testament, God in history, God in the formulations of theology and philosophy, becomes an object for human scrutiny and analysis. The important thing is to discriminate between true and false conceptions of God and to arrive at the truest possible conception of him. Such investigations are necessary and important and have profit in them if it is remembered that we have no valid criterion of true and false in regard to God unless God himself in his truth and love and justice and mercy is known to us as the living God with whom we have to do in all things in our life. But when God or the experience of God is analyzed as though God were a corpse on the dissecting table of the theological anatomist, there is an element of blasphemy in the procedure. God must remain God, in his freedom to hide himself or to reveal himself in all our speaking of him. He is not at the disposal of even the most expert theologian; nor is knowledge of him under any human control.

Perhaps the point at which in theology the mystery is most commonly denied is in anthropology. Even some who would acknowledge the mystery of God may proceed as though there were no impenetrable mystery concerning man. Psychology, sociology, and history have laid bare to us the nature of man. To know who he is we have only to read the objective evidence. Even man's sin may be rationally defined and documented, so that without any hearing of the gospel or any revelation of God it should be possible to secure from any man the confession that he is a sinner. But this whole viewpoint proceeds from a total unawareness of what the Scriptures mean by " man " and " sin." Just as the mystery of Jesus Christ was his relation with the

Father, so the mystery of every man is his relation with God. He is not an isolated person and can never be an isolated person, however hard he tries, because he is God's creature with the structure of his life, however perverted it may be, determined by his creaturely relation to God. But this relation may be so concealed that it fails to register on the charts of the psychologists and sociologists except as a puzzling vacancy. Who the man is can be known not by observation but only by revelation and faith. So also is sin a mystery that is revealed only when God is revealed. Anxiety, alienation, entanglement, personal and social irresponsibility or offensiveness, may all be objectively defined, so that a man is made to say, " I am anxious; I am alienated; I am entangled; I have done wrong." But sin, according to both Old and New Testaments, is in its ultimate nature a rupture of the relation between God and man. Its bitterest consequence is the darkness into which man falls when he is cut off from God. Therefore, a man can know that he is a sinner only within the context of the knowledge that he belongs in fellowship with God. That is why it is not the demonstration of the fact of his sin, but rather the work of mercy in which he knows himself accepted of God in spite of his sin, that enables a man to make the confession that he is a sinner. No teacher, however wise, can communicate that essential knowledge to him directly. He can know it only as he knows himself in the light of God.

Character-education programs are singularly blind to this truth. Their appeal is that they offer what seems to be a scientifically developed program for securing a well-balanced growth in Christian character in children and young people. There can be no question that psychology and educational technology have devised means whereby they can control character changes in human beings. It was used extensively in wartime to change quiet peace-loving young men into ferocious fighting men. There are similar techniques for the conditioning of dogs in order to make them safe, dependable guides for blind people or man-eating watchdogs. When one of our enemies uses these techniques, we call it " brainwashing " and shudder at the barbarism of it. Arthur

Koestler gives an excellent picture of their subtle and effective operation in his novel *Darkness at Noon*. But we remain unaware that the basic idea in a somewhat different form is powerfully influential in our own land. At the time of the death of John Dewey, Boyd H. Bode wrote in a magazine article that educators had now at their disposal the means of shaping human character in whatever direction might seem desirable and that if educators were not hampered by the persistence of traditional superstitions, they could speedily rid the world of most of its evils and could most certainly eliminate from human character the elements that are responsible for wars. Charles Morgan, in one of his essays in *Liberties of the Mind* tells how he was suddenly shocked awake to the peril of modern man when an American friend calmly informed him that science has now the power to control men's inmost convictions and attitudes in order to make them the kind of men that the supreme authority in the community desires for its service.

This is not just blasphemy; it is a threat to humanity worse by far than anything the world has ever known, more dangerous to the future of mankind than the atomic bomb, for the bomb can destroy only the bodies of men. "Fear not them which kill the body, but are not able to kill the soul: but rather fear him which is able to destroy both soul and body in hell." The Christian educator is tempted to think that he can take over this methodology and make it serve a Christian purpose, using it to create Christian character. But he has forgotten who a Christian is — that he is not just a person with certain superior qualities of character, since that could just as easily be a Pharisee and not a Christian, but a person who in confrontation with Jesus Christ has come to know God in his judgment and mercy and whose graces and gifts of character are all of them the fruits of God's Spirit. There are no scientific techniques for producing that kind of human being. As a *Christian* educator, then, he has to protest with all his strength against the blasphemy of any science that deals with man not as a child of God but as a complex of animal impulses and reflexes to be manipulated and conditioned at will. There is a similar temptation in evangelism, of men thinking they have discovered a technique by which they can manipulate human beings for their own good in order to secure from them "decisions for God." When the church plays with this thing, it should know that it is walking on the edge of the pit of hell.

One final illustration of this temptation to blasphemy is the claim that is made at times by educators that they can give children or young people an experience of God. Again there can be no question that a cleverly arranged service of worship can produce, in some at least of those taking part, a moving religious experience. By the association of certain symbols with these experiences they can be channeled in particular directions. The experiences can be most thrilling and memorable. But is not the very danger that the child or youth may really believe that this is what it means to have a Christian experience of God? In modern times there have been nations where the youth leaders have known how to generate in children and young people profoundly moving spiritual experiences in the context of a nationalistic religion. Also, medicine men in primitive societies were singularly adept in creating in men's minds a consciousness of the presence of divine powers. But what has the church of Jesus Christ to do with such blasphemy as this? We have no power to give men or women or children experiences of God. God is known only where he makes himself known in his Word and Spirit. We can bear witness to his Word, and we can wait in penitence and hope for him to come to us in his Spirit. But experiences of God are not ours to give. Only an education that has lost sight of the mystery of the gospel could make such a claim.

It is evident, then, that serious consequences ensue from any splitting asunder of the ministry of Jesus Christ. Each of its functions is essential to the others if they are not to develop in a perverse and unchristian form. Whether we are preachers or pastors or teachers, our ministry must be the whole ministry of Jesus Christ.

5

THE MINISTER AS PASTOR

BOTH theoretically and practically the situation in the area of pastoral work is confused and uncertain at present. Far too much of what has been written and spoken concerning the pastor has assumed that everyone knows what it means to be one and that what is needed by most men is merely inspiration and a few practical hints from a more experienced practitioner on how to improve one's technique. The confusion and uncertainty, however, have their source at a deeper level, in the failure to understand in what way the pastoral function belongs to the essential nature of the ministry and how it is related to the other primary functions of the ministry. Our concern therefore, will be chiefly with theological clarification at this point and many interesting and important aspects of the pastoral task will of necessity receive little attention.

One who ventures into this area without being a specialist in it is in serious danger of going astray, for he has to sail an uncharted course. While there is an abundance of literature on various practical aspects of the pastoral task, there is a remarkable scarcity of writings that explore the theological issues that must be brought into the open if practical decisions are to be made intelligently. As in other departments of practical theology such as homiletics and Christian education, the emphasis in the past has been on the practice rather than on the theology. The idea has long, too long, prevailed that these so-called practical departments do not require the same thorough theological investigation and development that is taken for granted in other departments such as Biblical interpretation, systematic theology, and church history.

In Christian education it has been considered very important to know educational theory and techniques, but theology has not been so essential; in fact, until recently a Christian educator could get by with very little theology. In homiletics, very widely the important thing has been to be expert in the preparation and delivery of sermons, and the expectation has been that the theological content of the sermons would be taken care of in other departments of the seminary. So also in pastoral theology, the emphasis has not been on theology but rather on the learning of techniques in the work of the parish. The consequence has been that in all three divisions of practical theology the literature for a long time has tended to be functional rather than theological, and that often there has been an embarrassing question mark hanging over the practical disciplines in our seminaries concerning their right to call themselves in the full sense *theological* disciplines. Paul Tillich, in his *Systematic Theology,* seems to locate the practical disciplines outside the structure of theology proper as constituting a kind of trade school in which the techniques of the ministry are learned. We may object to that, but we must recognize that it merely codifies an order that we have permitted to exist for far too long.

This order has had serious consequences in the life of the church. The lack of thorough theological investigation in these practical fields has left them open to confusion. The Niebuhr-Williams report on the ministry and theological education, as we mentioned earlier, states unequivocally that American Protestantism has no clear conception what the ministry is and that in every denomination there are widely varying conceptions in competition with one another. But is that confusion surprising when we search through the literature on the ministry and find not one competent volume that deals with the Biblical and theological foundations of homiletics or of the pastoral ministry? Or consider the chaotic state of affairs in religious education only a few years ago. Harrison Elliott's *Can Religious Education Be Christian?* published as recently as 1940, vehemently repudiated theological concern as an intruder in the area of religious education and called for a radical break with the whole historic theological tradition of the church. John Dewey was to be more significant for future developments than John the Apostle or John Calvin. For lack of a seriously critical theological self-scrutiny, religious education came very close to losing itself in a confusion of humanistic philosophy with Christianity. But in fairness to the religious educators we must ask, Is there any less confusion in our American preaching? And is this confusion unrelated to the fact that there has been a neglect of critical theological investigation and definition in homiletics? We have stumbled into chaos in our engrossment with practical and technical concerns.

In pastoral theology we find the same confusion and the same theological neglect. What does it mean to be a pastor? There is an evangelistic conception that says that the minister must preach the gospel from house to house and attempt the conversion of people as individuals and not just in the mass. There is a less evangelistic but religiously formal conception that merely insists that a minister read and pray, that is, conduct worship, regularly in the homes of his people. It is possible that these two conceptions belong largely to the past. Then there is the friendly church-visitor conception based on the principle that a home-going minister makes a church going people. There are men who make ten-minute calls in every home every six months and thereby keep their people under a sense of obligation to go to church. The content of the call is quite secondary; in ten minutes no serious conversation on any subject can be expected; but the technique is considered effective if it keeps the people under obligation. More recently there has been the counselor conception in which often general visitation of a congregation is abandoned and people with problems are encouraged to visit the minister in his study. This has the virtue of focusing the attention on problem cases where the need is greatest, and it is only natural that psychology, psychiatry, and psychoanalysis have been drawn into consideration to contribute what help they can in ministering to such people. But the tendency has been for this counseling task to be regarded as the whole pastoral task and for the term "counselor" to replace that of "pastor." Taking the picture as a whole, is it any wonder that the young graduate is not too clear in his mind about his pastoral office? The picture is confused, and far too little has been done to clear a path through the confusion.

There has been one courageous attempt to provide a theological preface to pastoral theology by Seward Hiltner (*Preface to Pastoral Theology,* Abingdon Press, 1958). He acknowledges the pioneer character of his work. Most American works published on the subject, Hiltner asserts, have been mere "hints and helps for ministers." Unfortunately Hiltner himself does not set his subject in its full theological context but proceeds from a viewpoint limited severely by his own concentration upon the development of the counseling aspect. He never once attempts to make clear what the total ministry is of which the pastoral office is one aspect or to show what relation a pastoral ministry in the present day has to the pastoral ministry of the prophets or of Jesus or of Paul. The result is that he leaves us still in our confusion concerning our responsibility and opportunity as pastors, and concerning the relation of the pastoral function to that of preaching and that of teaching.

One of the drastic needs of the present is clearly the recovery by the practical disciplines of their thoroughgoing theological character. In a later chapter we shall define the task of theology as the investigation of the question of truth and error in every aspect of the church's life. It is possible for the church so to preach, so to teach, so to act, so to deal with individuals, that it is no longer the church of Jesus Christ but something else, some other kind of institution. The church is in constant danger of unconsciously becoming something other than that which it was founded to be, the body of Jesus Christ, in which he continues to live and speak and act among men. To be a theologian in education is therefore to ask whether what we are doing educationally is in its central features and in all its details what we are compelled to do in faithfulness to the gospel of Jesus Christ. To be a theologian in homiletics is to ask what we must preach and how, if in our preaching Jesus Christ is himself to be present proclaiming the nearness of his Kingdom and offering himself to men as their only rightful King and Lord. And to be a theologian in pastoral theology is to ask what we must do and what we must not do in our dealing with individuals if our ministry to them is to be in the truest sense a continuation of the pastoral ministry of Jesus Christ himself. That question forces us back into the Scriptures to ask concerning the origins of a pastoral ministry. It makes us trace its varied formulations through the centuries in the church, trying always to see which developments were valid and which invalid. It makes us reconsider our doctrinal formulations of the Christian faith to find what it is in our understanding or misunderstanding of the gospel that empowers or incapacitates us for the pastoral office. Thus pastoral theology should be simply the bringing of the whole of theology to a focus upon this one point in the church's life where it attempts to deal with human beings not in the mass but as individuals or in intimate groups, family or otherwise.

The Complexity of the Problem

There are several other factors in the situation that should be mentioned at this point. In contrast to the counseling programs that require large amounts of time to be spent with people who have acute problems, is a tendency, encouraged by our American accent on bigness, to be impatient with spending time on individuals or small groups. It seems to be more efficient to use the available time to reach people on a broader scale. It is very easy for us, in a day when numbers are considered so important, to become blind to the opportunity that we have at no other time than when we are confronted with a single person and to forget that the church is built not by sweeping masses of people into it but by the awakening of faith in individuals, one by one. The mood of our day is against the expenditure of time on careful, painstaking pastoral work. But it is equally true that humanity in our day is acutely in need of pastoral care for this very reason, that individuals feel themselves lost in the impersonal mass of modern society. They are conscious of being manipulated in the mass by the clever advertisers of cigarettes, deodorants, and all the rest, and they are caught up into a mechanical round of activities both inside and outside the home in which there is little that is distinctively their own. They are in danger of becoming units in a mass society rather than persons. And even in the church there is constant danger that they may be nameless units in a mass rather than persons in a community. This is one reason why it is so important today for a minister to know his people's names, and not just those of the adults but also those of the children. It is well for him to know much more than the name, but certainly it is true that to be called by name always brings a sense of being recognized as a person. To be nameless in a community is to be a unit and not a person. One of the important functions of pastoral work is to transform an aggregation of units into a community of persons.

Part of this same problem is the fact that many people have no one either in the home or among their friends with whom they can discuss freely doubts or difficulties that they have in relation to the Christian faith or questions that trouble them at the very center of their existence. The more important the matters are, the less likelihood is there of their having anyone from whom they can expect even a patient and sympathetic hearing. The Christian church should be a fellowship in which they would find the opportunity they need and would be able to bring their questions into the open, but only too often the fellowship that one finds in the church remains on too superficial a level. It is imperative, therefore, that the minister make himself available to his people at this point of need, establishing in their minds the confidence that they can open to him freely any question that may be of concern to them. That confidence is not built in a moment, and it is never built unless the minister struggles against the current tendency to spend his time with his people in friendly but superficial and purposeless conversation.

For some ministers the development of a counseling program, or it may be merely the development of a program that stops short of counseling, has meant the abandonment of all attempts to visit in the homes of their people. The minister is available in his study at certain hours for persons who need his help. Beyond this he visits the sick and the dying and persons in special need. In this way his time seems to be used to best advantage. A program of home-to-home visitation, he says, is too wasteful of time and can so easily be merely a succession of social calls, expected by the people but not intended by them to have any spiritual significance. Moreover, if the calls are made in the afternoon, he sees only the woman of the house, and it is a bit unmanly for a minister to spend his afternoons visiting with the women of the congregation.

In defending a measure of home-to-home visitation, it needs to be made very clear that it is an insufferable bondage when a minister feels compelled to call in each home once in every so many months. That may be a major impediment to any effective pastoral ministry. Purposeless calling is likely to be a fruitless occupation. But when the minister ceases to go into the homes of his people and meets them at close quarters only on special occasions or when their problems become sufficiently acute to make them seek him out in his study, there are serious losses involved. First, there is a narrowing of his pastoral ministry to the acute problem cases, so that he ceases to get near the host of others with less acute but no less real and important problems. Secondly, there is a misunderstanding of the pastoral office as though its one concern were with peoples' special problems. The pastoral function should have in it as many concerns as there are in the total ministry of Jesus Christ. There are times when in pastoral conversation the need is to tell the person plainly and convincingly what the gospel has to say to him, in short, to preach the gospel — but woe betide the pastor who preaches to an individual as though he were addressing a congregation. More often there are opportunities for teaching, though again it should be in such a form that the person is unaware that he is being taught. To him it will be merely an interesting and profitable conversation but to the minister it will be a part of his teaching ministry. Both the preaching and the teaching ministries need to be brought to bear upon the pastoral ministry in order to give it content and purpose. It is not sufficient to do our preaching in the pulpit and our teaching in classes in the church. We need to go to people where they are living and in conversation with them take up our ministry to them so that we speak in direct relation to the questions and problems that arise at their present growing point in the Christian faith. It is in such conversations that they will discover their dilemmas and difficulties to us before they become acute. This broader type of pastoral care we might liken to preventative medicine, by which the spiritual health of our people is maintained and guarded. If there were more of it being practiced, there would be fewer acute problem cases demanding special attention.

Sufficient has been said to indicate the complexity of the problem that confronts us and the need for a rethinking of the nature of the pastoral office. The starting point for any such rethinking should be an examination of the nature of the ministry in the Scriptures but particularly as it finds its definitive expression in Jesus Christ.

THE PASTORAL MINISTRY IN THE SCRIPTURES

Already in the Old Testament the lines of a pastoral ministry begin to appear. The earliest function of the priest we have seen to be the giving of Torah, which is not just law but also direction and instruction. The priest was the custodian of the nation's religious tradition; to him the people were supposed to be able to turn for understanding and guidance in all problems that involved their relationship with God and with each other. To Hosea the irresponsibility of the priests was that they themselves no longer had any true knowledge of the God in whose name they ministered. Also the prophet shared in the pastoral care of the community. We usually think of the prophet as thundering his messages of doom at the nation as a whole rather than as dealing with individuals — a preacher rather than a pastor. But if we look more closely, we find that, even though the public oracles are invariably directed to the nation, there are clear indications of the prophet's concern with individuals. Isaiah had a group of disciples with whom he was intimately concerned. Jeremiah thinks of prophets and priests as physicians whose task is to heal the wound in the nation's life (Jer. 6:13-14). Ezekiel describes the prophet as a shepherd and watchman over the community who is responsible to God for the life of each member of the community (Ezek. 3:16 ff.). It is in Second Isaiah, however, that the pastoral concern of the prophet comes to clearest expression. He describes himself in Isa. 50:4 ff. as listening each morning for a word from God with which to strengthen the fainting courage of his people. There is evidence at various points in his book of a group of believers clustered about him and looking to him for guidance and help. There is evidence also that, where he found his people unfaithful to God, he had no hesitation in pointing out to them where they were going astray, and so earned the enmity of some of them in return for his care of them.

In the ministry of Jesus this focus upon individuals comes into much greater prominence, so much so that sometimes his prophetic mission to the nation as a whole is lost from sight. If we examine the material in the Gospels that formed the substance of Jesus' preaching and teaching, we shall find a large part of it with the stamp upon it not of addresses to large audiences but rather of conversations with individuals and small groups. Much of the material in the Sermon on the Mount is best understood as having been addressed to a group of committed disciples rather than to a mixed multitude. The Gospels are full of incidents where Jesus is represented as speaking to one or two people. Take out of the Gospels all the passages in which Jesus is acting as pastor and there would be a great void.

It is also plain that Jesus thought of himself as pastor. In one familiar passage he describes himself as a physician, sent not to all men indiscriminately but to the sick, and therefore justified in going only to those who need him most. John's Gospel represents him as calling himself " the good shepherd " and as not only knowing each of his sheep by name but also as being known by each of them. It is one thing for the pastor to know his people; it is something different, something much more important and much more costly to him, to let himself be known to them. Jesus' pastoral relationship with his disciples and with others was one in which he laid himself open to them in an unconditional way, interpenetrated their situation with his love and understanding, and took upon himself the burden of their sins, distresses, and anxieties. He gave himself to them, not in any sentimental way, but in the profoundest identification of himself with them. He made himself one with them, so that they were conscious of his not judging them from without but understanding them from within.

The striking feature, however, in almost all accounts of Jesus' pastoral dealings with individuals is that the profundity of his understanding is accompanied by what can only be called a drastic surgical approach to the person's problem. The rich young ruler approached Jesus with great respect and with a frank admission that his highly moral and religious achievement was insufficient, but Jesus, probing to the root of his problem, which was the ultimate mastery of his soul by his love of his possessions, made him choose between God and possessions. Nicodemus, a learned man, when he engaged Jesus in conversation, was abruptly confronted with the ultimatum that no man could know anything of God's Kingdom unless he was born of the Spirit. With Zacchaeus a transformation was effected simply by Jesus' acceptance of him in a situation where he was experiencing rejection from all his fellow townsmen. Simon the Pharisee, in Luke 7:35 ff., heard from Jesus a parable that told him that he was nothing more than a bankrupt with God and that his failure to recognize his dependence upon God's mercy made him a merciless and loveless man. The lawyer who asked Jesus to define a neighbor received an answer in the parable of the good Samaritan that must have left him gasping and angry. The general impression is that Jesus' public relations methods were not in the best modern tradition. He was not concerned primarily with keeping people friendly and loyal to him. By his abruptness and even offensiveness he must have lost many people like the rich young ruler from his movement who could have been won over and incorporated into the church by any modern pastor. The difference arises from the fact that so often today the aim of pastoral work is primarily to keep people friendly and loyal toward the church. Jesus' primary aim had to do with the relation of the person to God, the laying bare of the hidden obstacles to his true life in God, and the conquest of those obstacles. He preferred to lose the man for the time being rather than for the sake of a superficial friendliness and a deceptive intimacy to leave the man in the dark about himself. His first responsibility was to speak the truth to each man in love. In short, as a pastor he was discharging his full ministry in immediate confrontation with individuals, speaking to them in the most informal conversational way the word that had in it for them both God's judgment upon them and the power of God to redeem them.

Another feature of Jesus' pastoral ministry was his increasing focus on people who for some reason or other felt themselves excluded from the religious community. At the beginning of his ministry he is frequently reported present in the synagogue, but as the resistance of the religious community to his gospel grew, he turned more and more to the outsiders. The parable of the lost sheep, which was spoken in defense of that policy, reveals the direction of Jesus' concern. " I am not sent but unto the lost sheep of the house of Israel." His pastoral ministry was an active search for those who needed him most and who, by the absence of religious and moral defenses against his claims upon them, were most likely to respond to his approach. The ninety-nine sheep safely in the fold are plainly the good loyal respectable members of the synagogue. That Jesus considered them safe in God's fold can no more be deduced from the parable than that Jesus considered the Pharisees genuinely righteous and healthy can be deduced from Mark 2:17. The exact opposite is evident in the parable told by Jesus to Simon the Pharisee in Luke 7:41. To Jesus all men were sick and sinful and therefore in need of pardon and healing from God. But until men knew they were sick and sinful he could do little for them. He found the outsiders much more ready to acknowledge their need. It is important also that Jesus went in search of those who needed him and did not wait for them to come to him. This characteristic of his mission, which is of such significance for the entire outlook of the church, was rooted in the nature of the love of God, which must invade the world in search of the objects of its care. Jesus was a pastor not just because he was interested in people or because it was a way of attaching people to his movement but because he could not be the One in whom God's saving love dwelt in all its fullness without being constantly a shepherd hunting through the highways and byways of Palestine for his lost sheep.

IMPLICATIONS FOR THE SHAPING OF THE MODERN PASTORAL MINISTRY

It would carry us too far afield to consider passages bearing on the pastoral office in the remainder of the New Testament. As it is, we have made only a sampling of evidence from the Gospels. But the sampling is sufficient to suggest to us that our current conceptions of a pastor are not very closely in line with what we see in the Gospels and that our rethinking can profitably find its starting point in the Scriptures. A few specific points stand out most prominently.

First, the word "pastor" has behind it both for Jesus and for the prophets the concept of shepherd, and in Old and New Testaments alike the shepherd's responsibility is not limited in any narrow way. Ezekiel and Second Isaiah as prophet-shepherds in Israel regarded the whole nation as being under their care. Both undoubtedly had groups of believing disciples who clustered about them and profited most from their ministries, but they felt themselves responsible to God even for those who were hostile to them. Jesus, as we have seen, took as his special task of shepherding the reaching of those within the nation who had placed themselves beyond the pale of religion, but there can be no question that all Israel belonged within the flock that he sought to gather under his care. Contrast with that the way in which the work of a pastor is today conceived as the exercising of a personal care over the members of a Christian congregation, the visiting of the sick, the aged, the bereaved, or those in any special trouble. If the congregation has a large membership, these duties engross a large part of the minister's time, and if he attempts a yearly house-to-house visitation, it absorbs all his available time for pastoral work. Thus he finds himself in the disturbing situation of being a shepherd who, in contradiction to Jesus' parable of the lost sheep, spends all his time, and is expected to spend all his time, in the care of the ninety and nine who are safely in the fold (or at least so consider themselves) and has no time whatsoever to follow Jesus in his pastoral search for lost sheep. Being a good pastor only too easily comes to mean taking such good care of the members of one's congregation that they remain loyal and are not inclined to stray away into other folds where the pastor may be more attentive. At this point there is need for revolution today in the name of Jesus Christ. Congregations need to be told how Jesus defined a pastor and that their congregational life should be so organized and the attitude of the people such that the minister can be liberated to lead the way for others in search of lost sheep in the world outside the church.

That suggests a second step. The pastoral task both inside and outside the church, for we dare not overlook either area, is so vast that in no community can the work be overtaken by one man. It has been proved in the past that every congregation has in it men and women who, with training, can do very effective pastoral work. It is absolute folly for all the shepherding to be left to one person. We should follow Jesus' example in training the Twelve and then the Seventy to share the work with him, building up in each congregation a body of men and women who will be willing to take careful training and to spend themselves in this essential ministry. Only when that happens are minister and people likely to find their way over the wall of the religious community into the world outside where the greatest opportunity lies.

Another point at which Jesus' example sets our practices in question is in the way in which he discharges his full ministry in the pastoral situation. In his dealings with individuals he is both preacher and teacher. He preaches and teaches in a conversational manner that in a measure conceals what he is doing, but nevertheless it is singularly effective preaching and teaching. He does not, as pastor, do something quite different from what he is doing in his public ministry. It is here that often today there is a radical discontinuity in our ministries. The preacher and the pastor can be two quite different people. At a ministers' conference some years ago one man spoke for many when he confessed that he could preach the gospel fluently as long as he had a pulpit between himself and his people, but when that formal situation was no longer there and he found himself informally confronted with one of his people, he was tongue-tied and helpless, without a word to say.

There is no severer test in the ministry than that which meets us in the pastoral situation. It tests the integrity of our knowledge, for while secondhand knowledge, and even secondhand sermons, can sometimes be passed off for the real thing in the pulpit, in personal conversation, eye to eye, we can speak only that which we know for ourselves. It also tests the strength of our understanding and concern in relation to our people when we have to deal not with human problems in general but with the specific problem of one person.

So severe and shattering is this test when we first meet it that it is only human that we should try to run away from it. There are various forms of evasion. One is the finding of good reasons for abandoning all visitation in homes. Another is the shortening of the visit to a period so brief that no significant conversation is possible. Another is the resolute maintenance of a chatty, superficial level in the interview that effectively discourages serious questions. Yet another is the formal religious visit that gives the minister a good conscience that he has done something to make the call religious when in actuality he as a pastor has gone into hiding behind his Bible-reading and prayer. There are innumerable ways of guarding ourselves against costly exposure to the rude realities of our people's lives. But when we refuse all such protection and accept this exposed position as the necessary permanent condition of our ministry, it has profound consequences not only for our pastoral work but also for our preaching and teaching. The pastoral situation becomes for us the place where we learn who the people are to whom we preach on Sunday and whom we teach on Thursday. In fact, our preaching becomes a continuation in public of the conversations we have been having in private and retains the quality of personal address in which we seek to speak the word that we have heard for ourselves in the Scriptures in which God himself deals in judgment and in mercy with our broken, confused, sinful lives.

This continuity of the preaching and pastoral ministries is extremely important in dealing with people who have special problems. Quite often the problem has its origin in an arrested spiritual development. The person is failing in the relationships of life because he has no more than a twelve-year-old's understanding of the Christian faith and has no knowledge of the resources of prayer. What he needs is help in discovering the realities of his situation and in taking the first steps in an independent development in faith and prayer. What must not happen is that he should develop a relation of dependence upon the minister rather than upon God. He should therefore at the earliest possible moment find in the worship and sermons of the sanctuary the continuation of what began for him in the private conversation. This point is significant in the light of the tendency in some forms of counseling to attach the person to the minister as counselor and to prolong the private interviews over a wide expanse of time.

Finally, the entire pastoral ministry is to be undertaken in full awareness that no person receives a Christian ministry in the midst of his problems and distresses unless somehow his life is brought under the light of God's own presence. We are ministers of God before we are ministers to human need, and our one hope that something effective may be accomplished concerning the problems of our people is that through our ministry they may become aware of *God's* dealing with them, that is, aware that at the root of their problem is something wrong in their relationship with God and that the beginning of healing in their practical problems is the healing and restoration of this inner relationship. We dare not lead them to think that there is something we can do, some word we can speak as ministers, some discipline we can lay upon them, some process of counseling to which we can submit them, that of itself is able to accomplish the desired healing. There *are* things that men can do to help people in their troubles; that has been proved by the psychologists, psychiatrists, and psychoanalysts; but the help given from these quarters does not claim to be and cannot be the kind of help that comes only from reconciliation with God. It will be a tragic thing if Christian ministers begin to forget that they are ministers of reconciliation in this radical sense that we see exemplified in Jesus' own ministry, and exchange this ministry for one that, by copying some of the techniques of the psychiatrists, seems to offer people more direct and immediate help. We need to learn all that we can from psychology, psychiatry, and psychoanalysis to deepen our understanding of the people with whom we deal and to guard ourselves against approaches to them that are likely only to complicate their problems. A minister who refuses to learn from these sciences is as irresponsible in his work as a pastor as he would be as preacher and teacher if he refused to make use of the Biblical researches of the past two hundred years in his interpretation of the Bible. We need every help we can find in lifting the edge of darkness that always hides the other person from us. But what must not happen is that the Christian minister exchange the role of minister of reconciliation for the role of a species of amateur psychiatrist. The two are not just the ancient and the modern forms of the same thing.

The pastor, however much he may be helped from many modern sources in his understanding of his people, is not likely to be a minister of reconciliation to them unless he learns to read his own and their inner situation out of the Scriptures. The word of God in Scripture is not just a revelation of God; it is also a revelation of man, and these are not two separate revelations, but one. Wherever God reveals himself, man sees himself and his whole life in a new light. The point at which God reveals himself fully in Jesus Christ is the point at which the heights and depths of our humanity are laid bare. Not only the mystery of God but also the mystery of man is pierced by the Word of God. The Bible is therefore the primary textbook of the pastor out of which he reads his people, their problems, and the way of their healing. By it he will be kept from all superficial diagnoses of even the least of their problems, for he will learn that what shows as only a tiny problem on the surface may be the only visible evidence of a much larger and deeper problem in the person's life with God. The rich young ruler thought he lacked only some one small thing in his spiritual life when in actuality he had not yet faced the magnitude of the No! that he was saying to God. But, above all, the Scriptures keep us aware that the problems of any one man are not in himself alone or merely in his relations with one or two people, so that if he is twisted in himself or tangled in his relation with others, we can get him straightened out. The deepest reality of his life is his relation with God, and this is the substructure of his relations with himself and with those about him. Therefore, all our straightening out of relations with himself and others leaves the main problem untouched, so that at the center, in his relation with God, a conflict remains out of which at any moment may emerge disruptive forces. He is not really helped until at the center he is reconciled with God. But this is not something that we or anyone else can accomplish with human techniques. The ultimately decisive help is not ours but God's. The Word and Spirit of God are his only hope. This is what makes the ministry of the Word and Spirit of such paramount importance. God uses a human ministry that men in the midst of their present problems and distresses may hear God himself speaking to them in his Word and may know themselves confronted with God himself in his Spirit.

Some years ago Eduard Thurneysen, until recently minister of the Cathedral and professor of homiletics in Basel, published an article on " Justification by Faith and the Pastor's Task " in which he warned the ministry against raising false expectations in people's minds. Only too easily do people begin to think that we as pastors can solve their problems for them, and this impression is reinforced when they hear from a number of people that a certain minister has been most successful in solving people's problems. Some ministers begin even to be advertised as experts in this respect. Thurneysen pointed out that if justification by faith is the ultimate need of each of these people, we dare not do anything that will lead them to trust in solutions of their problems on a more superficial level. Our task before all else is to get them to see the real problem of their existence, which is hidden behind the complex of difficulties visible to them. This is another way of saying that we must be ministers of God to them, bringing to them the good news that God has acted decisively to meet the real problem of their lives, so that they must give up all attempts to find some lesser form of justification for themselves and receive as a gift from God his justification of them in Jesus Christ. A pastoral ministry of this kind is much more exacting and dangerous than any other kind, but it can be undertaken with the confidence that in it we are beginning to share in the pastoral ministry of our Lord himself.

6

THE MINISTER AS THEOLOGIAN

WHY AN EDUCATED MINISTRY?

IN most churches it is the established order that candidates for an ordained ministry should receive an extensive education, first in the arts and sciences and then in theology. It seems obvious that men and women who are to serve the church well must have an education that enables them to take their places intelligently in any company and to explore the relations of their own special subject to other areas of human interest and concern, and equally obvious that they should have a thorough introduction to the life and thought of the church. But the necessity has not always been recognized, and it dare not be assumed that the candidate for the ministry sees the why of it. Until late in the nineteenth century in England no special theological training was required for ordination, many men in the ministry having only a general classical education. There are churches today in which a call to the ministry is recognized as a sufficient basis for ordination, and the amount of education that is received depends more upon the individual's inclination than upon any strict requirements of the church. The trend, however, in all denominations is toward higher standards of education and more intensive theological training.

It might seem at this point that the concept, thus far developed, of a ministry that in the most thoroughgoing way is based on the ministry as it appears in Scripture, offers a very weak rationale for the church's insistence upon high educational standards and

123

years of theological preparation. In the Old Testament the priests seem to have received their training in a long apprenticeship in the Temple or shrine itself. The prophetic guilds would undoubtedly have procedures for the incorporation of new members into the guild, but their possession by the Spirit of God was the essential thing. The great prophets seemed to take up their office directly upon receiving a call of God. However, their writings show them to be men of the finest culture, able to express themselves in noble poetic forms and with a breadth of outlook that is often remarkable. Amos is sometimes represented as a rough, uneducated peasant farmer who suddenly at God's call becomes a prophet to Israel, but any careful study of his language and thought reveals him to be steeped in the religious traditions of his nation, a poet of unusual power, and by any standard a well-educated man. We do not know who were the authors and editors of many of the books of the Old Testament, repeating and reinterpreting the traditions of centuries, but when we compare their products even from a purely literary standpoint with other records from the ancient world, we recognize the distinction of their achievement. We do not know who wrote the psalms, but we can discern a hard gemlike quality in the language of many of them, a perfection of simplicity, that comes not from the untrained mind but only from the most highly disciplined. Whatever estimate one makes of the author of Ecclesiastes, one is not likely to think him an uneducated man. And the writings of Second Isaiah and of the author of The Book of Job have in them a quality that impresses even those who do not share the faith that they express.

In the New Testament we are confronted at once by the fact that Jesus himself was by trade a carpenter and that there is no indication of his having had special training for a religious vocation. The Gospels describe him as breaking off his occupation in Nazareth to visit John the Baptist, as receiving the call to his ministry at the time of his baptism by John, and as beginning his ministry after a brief interval. He may at times have been given the title "rabbi" as a religious teacher or the title "prophet" because of the similarity of his preaching to that of the prophets, but the evidence is against his having received training in the rabbinic schools, and, apart from the community of John the Baptist, there was no opportunity in his time for apprenticeship in a prophetic vocation. Yet these facts cannot be used to describe Jesus as an uneducated man. It is absurd to equate education with graduation from an educational institution. Education has to do with the mental and spiritual development of a person and his competence to think and act effectively in his vocation. Luke tells us that Jesus had an education, that he had to grow in wisdom as well as in stature, and in favor with God as well as in favor with men, but we tend to fall into a Docetism in our thinking of him and to ignore what was involved humanly in his attaining the discipline of mind that could express itself on the spur of the moment in absolutely perfect gems such as the parable of the good Samaritan in Luke 10:25 ff. or the parable of the two debtors in ch. 7:41-42. Jesus may not have been to the right schools of his day, but not only was he a highly educated person but he was an educator of most penetrating insight. It is still rewarding in spite of all the advances and discoveries of modern education to study the methods that are implicit in his approach to men. One instance, superbly developed by R. J. McCracken in a broadcast sermon, is Jesus' refusal often to give a direct answer to men's questions, forcing them instead to face the realities of their situation and to find the answer for themselves. We are likely to attribute such competence in teaching and the ability to express what was in his mind with such perfectness in memorable words and sentences to Jesus' divinity rather than to a humanity that was subject to education and growth. It is no denial of Jesus' divinity to assert that his words give evidence of one of the most disciplined minds that has been known in the history of the human race.

What, then, of the disciples? Were not some of them rough fishermen? Is there not a valid witness in Acts 4:13 that they were "uneducated, common men"? They heard the call of Jesus to share his mission and after only a brief training were sent out two by two into the towns and villages of Galilee. What was essential was that they themselves had heard the gospel from the lips of Jesus, had known through him the forgiveness of their sins and the beginning of a new life with God, and had been chosen by him to declare the gospel to others. What more was necessary? The suspicion that educational and theological disciplines are not essential to an evangelical ministry but are actually an intrusion of human requirements into what should be wholly a divine preparation is likely to have its strongest support in the example of the disciples. But again there has been an unwarranted emphasis upon the rude simplicity of the disciples. The members of the Sanhedrin in Acts 4:13 are amazed at the ability of the disciples to express themselves since they plainly had not received an education in the schools such as was customary for anyone exercising religious leadership. The verse is testimony, therefore, not to the rudeness of the disciples, but rather to a remarkable and impressive ability evident in them that had not been learned in the schools of religion. The fact that a man was a fisherman or a carpenter or a shepherd in Palestine dare not be made the basis for an assumption that he was ignorant and uneducated. In the static Judaism of that day intelligent tradesmen could be much more readily trained for a ministry by Jesus than the most brilliant graduates of the religious schools. Whatever the quality of the disciples' previous development may have been (and concerning it we know nothing either positive or negative), they received from Jesus intensive training for their mission, and, if we are to judge by the competence of Peter that is evident in the early chapters of The Acts, by the time of Jesus' death they had an education that equipped them to be spokesmen of the gospel in any company.

Paul's description of his entry upon his apostleship in Gal., ch. 1, seems to leave no room for preparatory theological training. His conversion experience, in which Jesus appeared to him as he had to the other apostles, not only constituted him an apostle, so that he needed no further human authorization, but also gave him the gospel that he was to preach to the Gentiles.

The conversion was followed by a period in Arabia that is usually assumed to have been a time of preparation but whose purpose is totally unknown to us, and by three years in Damascus, during which apparently he was exercising his ministry to Gentiles. Following Paul's own account of his movements rather than that of the Acts, we learn that there was then a fifteen-day visit with Peter in Jerusalem before he launched out upon many years of mission in Asia Minor and Greece. And yet Paul was not only the great missionary pioneer in carrying the gospel to the Gentiles but also the great theological reinterpreter who translated the gospel into a new terminology that would give it freer access to the Gentile mind. No student of Paul's letters is likely to suggest that there was anything superficial either in his general education in two cultures, the Jewish and the Greek, or in his theological equipment for his mission. However he received it, the fact of it is indisputable. He undoubtedly had years of training in the rabbinical schools before he became a Christian, and there must have been many habits of thought that he had painfully to unlearn, but nevertheless there would be much in this earlier education that made its contribution to his later achievements. W. D. Davies, in *Paul and Rabbinic Judaism* (The Macmillan Company), provides a masterly study of the influence of Paul's rabbinic training upon his thinking and upon the way he formulated his gospel. Then, as a Christian he did not likely become at once the Paul whom we know from the letters. That he had his gospel from the risen Lord does not mean that he could have written the letter to the Romans with its elaboration of Christian doctrine during the first year of his ministry. We could say of Paul that his theological education was concurrent with his discharge of his apostleship. Its thoroughness is witnessed by the quality of the final product that has stood the test of centuries and provided a starting point and substance for innumerable ventures in theological reinterpretation.

The general conclusion from all these Biblical instances is twofold. They give no encouragement to anyone who desires to enter upon the Christian ministry without submitting to strenuous cultural disciplines. The Biblical exponents of the ministry, rather, move on a level of refinement in thinking, cultural competence, and mastery in the use of words that make us ashamed of our rudeness and incompetence even after the most careful preparation in our advanced schools. But at the same time the emphasis throughout the Bible is upon the indispensableness of a call from God, upon a faith and an understanding that are not to be gained in any school but are the gift of God's Spirit, and upon the simplicity of the task of ministry, that it is essentially a matter of bearing faithful witness in word and action to the judging, redeeming Word that has struck into the heart of one's own life. There can be no suggestion, then, that Spirit-endowment makes educational discipline unnecessary, for where we have in the Scriptures the surest evidence of Spirit-endowment we find minds that are unusually open to the problems of human life and active in the most disciplined way. It is significant that the earliest name for a believer, that is, for one who had received the baptism of the Spirit, was " disciple," which means learner or student.

WHY THEOLOGY?

There still remains the question why there need be the special disciplines of theology and a special theological preparation for the ministry. If in the Scriptures we have the record of God's saving acts by which he called the church into being and ever sustains it in being, and if the function of the church is to bear witness to him by declaring his saving acts both then and now, what need is there for theology? Can the church not live directly out of Scripture? Can the minister of the word not fulfill his responsibility by interpreting the message of the Scriptures to his people both in preaching and in teaching? What does the ordinary Christian need except his Bible and his prayers that he may be kept in closest fellowship with God? Is not the theologian an intruder who comes between the Bible and the church, the Bible and the minister, the Bible and the ordinary Christian? Moreover, what evidence is there of the people of God needing theologians in Old and New Testament times? Was it not a sounder order that they knew as they lived directly by the Word and Spirit of God and not by a Word and Spirit mediated through the confusing interpretations of a multitude of theologians? Was it not the confluence of the Christian stream of the gospel with the philosophical stream of the Greeks that lost for us the simplicity of the more ancient order and entangled us in the intellectual distinctions of theological discourse?

To this it must be answered that, even as education of an intensive and effective kind existed in ancient Israel under a form that is quite unfamiliar to us, so also did theological discourse and the making of theological distinctions. The book of Genesis looks to us like a storybook, vastly different in form from a volume of systematic theology, yet in its story form it deals with the profoundest theological issues. In ten words it may bring to expression a truth concerning the relation of God and man that will occupy the modern theologian for a hundred pages as he endeavors to understand it. The story of Creation in the first three chapters of Genesis is no child's story, but rather it embodies within itself some of the most important insights of Israel's faith, stating them with extreme care in order to avoid and counteract false beliefs that were widely current in the ancient world. The same is true wherever we turn in Scripture. The simplicity of the words (e.g., of the psalms or of the parables of Jesus) is deceptive for those who are unaware that simple words do not necessarily have a simple meaning. A whole lifetime of thoughtful living by faith in God in the midst of a dangerous world is distilled into the Twenty-third Psalm. The whole of Jesus' gospel is poured into the parable of the prodigal son. And the theological distinctions in both are razor-sharp. Theology did not begin when the Christians met the Greeks. That meeting forced it into new forms of expression and created problems for it that had not been faced in the same terms earlier, but it was in Israel, a nation whose very existence was grounded in a personal relation with God, that theology, which is literally the exploration of the meaning of God for life, received its earliest formulation.

The forms of expression that theology had in Israel are significant of its character. They are most of them in some way or other portions of a dialogue between God and man. This is only natural, since the whole of Israel's life within the covenant is a ceaseless dialogue with God, of which every happening, in the Temple, in the palace, in the market place, on the farms, on the battlefield, is an essential part. In the prophets and elsewhere we hear God speaking to his people, sometimes pleading with them, sometimes thundering at them in anger, but always in the one way or the other calling them in love to find their life in covenant with him. In the psalms we hear the response of Israel's faith to God in all its infinite variety of adoration, trust, repentance, thanksgiving, rebellion, submission, despair of self, rejoicing at deliverance. In the history books we have unfolded before our eyes with grim realism the tragic story of a nation torn between faith and self-assertion. In Job and Ecclesiastes, men of faith insist on looking with open eyes at what seem to them to be the realities of their situation and asking their painful questions of God. Theology is never a matter of intellectual abstractions in Israel because God and the realities of man's life are inseparable. God is known by them not with the mind alone but with the totality of their existence. They can never speak or even think of a man in isolation because man for them does not exist except in his relation with God. The relation may be one of covenant love or one of alienation, but whichever it is, it determines everything in life.

So also in the New Testament the whole of life is comprehended in theology, not theology as a subject of thought for scholars but theology as the mystery of how all things, all events, have their origin and meaning in the covenant relation between God and man. There have been writers who have called Jesus' teachings a simple, untheological gospel. There could be no greater nonsense. There is no word he spoke that does not have its significance as a revelation of God's dealings with man and man's dealings with God. In Jesus' person and words, in his death and resurrection, the dialogue between God and man reaches the simplicity and decisiveness of "last words." God speaks his final word to man in the person of Jesus, and most clearly in his death and resurrection; and in the same cross man speaks his final self-revealing word to God, the word in which is concentrated all his blindness and hatred and fear and rebellion. But another word is spoken in that same place in response to God, not a word by men but a word *for* men, on their behalf, a word they could never have spoken for themselves, Jesus' word of perfect love and obedience to the Father.

Theology, then, is inescapable for a church or a ministry that takes the Scriptures in earnest and seeks to spell out their meaning. There can be no interpretation of Scripture in any form, that is, interpretation that goes beyond the historical and literary to the living content of the text, that is not confronted at every step with theological questions and theological realities. The church from the very beginning has been involved in theological discussion as it has tried to understand what it means in each new age to be faithful to the gospel of Jesus Christ. One would expect that if there were any age in which all things would be so clear that there would be no reason for differences or controversy concerning the truth of the gospel, it would be in the earliest age of the church, directly after the death and resurrection of Jesus. And yet in that very age the church had to face one of its sharpest and bitterest theological debates. James, the brother of Jesus, and his Jerusalem colleagues were undoubtedly certain in their own minds that they were keeping the church faithful to the order of life that they had seen in Jesus when they insisted that Jewish Christians should observe the Jewish food laws and not eat with uncircumcised Gentiles. They could agree with Paul at many points concerning the gospel, but this point of difference they could not concede. Paul on his part saw the truth of the gospel at stake in the suggestion that faith of itself was insufficient to make a man a Christian, but that to faith must be added the observance of certain traditional Jewish practices. The letters to the Galatians and to the Romans, two of the church's greatest theological documents, were written by Paul to state what he held to be the truth in the matter.

Theology is a necessity, because we are a human church in which God is seen not face to face but as in a darkened mirror. The Scriptures speak of a day when it will be no longer necessary for anyone to say to his brother, "Know the Lord," for all will know him, a day when we shall know as we are known, but that is a day at the end of time and not in "the time between" where the church has its life. That Christians contradict one another concerning the truth of the gospel is not necessarily perversity, as so many have always seemed to think. The most serious differences have always been between men who are deeply in earnest and concerned above all to be loyal to their Lord. Theological discussion in its deepest intent is not just an attempt of each to overcome the other, and if there be any humble consciousness of how far beyond both theologians the truth in Christ is likely to be, it will not be a surprise to either to find himself overcome at points where he least expects. Theology exists in the church because of the recognition that as long as the world stands, the true gospel will be imperiled by false gospels even in its stanchest defenders. Therefore, the church owes a duty to its Lord to search out the truth with every means at its disposal and to sharpen in all its members, but particularly in its ministers, the ability to distinguish between the true gospel and the false.

The Minister as Theologian

These preliminary considerations have prepared the way for the statement of the thesis that a minister of Jesus Christ, in order to fulfill the functions of his ministry responsibly, must be a theologian. Theologians, according to the most widely prevalent manner of thinking, are professors in theological seminaries or young ministers who have taken extensive graduate training and are only temporarily in a parish until an opening comes for them in a seminary. Ministers think of themselves as preachers, teachers, pastors, counselors, administrators, but not as theologians. They may read a number of theological books each year, but they would in general draw back from the suggestion that they are theologians. A theologian to them is someone who is working critically and creatively at the shaping of the church's theology, and their own role in relation to theology they see as a passive rather than an active one. They depend upon the theologians for guidance and stimulus in their thinking, but their image of themselves does not include critical and creative theological work. Nor do the courts of the church consider theology to be an essential function of the church's ministry. If we were to examine the minutes of all the church courts, presbyteries, synods, assemblies, associations of churches, and church councils that have met in the past ten years, we would find in them a very scanty record of discussions of theological issues. Theology is not generally regarded as a practical matter or as an urgent concern demanding the time and attention of church courts.

That has not always been true. A book of rules and regulations for church order in Scotland, *The First Book of Discipline,* published originally four centuries ago, has in it a rule (long since forgotten) that on one Monday of each month the ministers of the presbytery should meet to hear a sermon by one of the brethren and to examine its doctrine in critical discussion. They were aware that nothing was more essential to the strength and health of the church than sound teaching, and they were convinced that ministers needed one another's help in order to escape from error into truth and to enlarge and deepen their understanding of the gospel. It may be true that some ministers might listen to their brothers' sermons with more eagerness to find error than truth and that the rule could be used to enforce a dull and deadly conformity, particularly upon younger ministers. But surely it is a more Christian order than the one that many ministers have experienced at the beginning of their ministries — inducted into a village congregation after a mere introduction to the Christian faith in seminary and left totally to themselves to sink or swim in the entire work of the ministry, periodic meetings with their fellow ministers to transact church business but with no opportunity to discuss the real problems of the church's existence in the realm of faith, or the problems of their own existence as ministers charged with the awesome task of speaking the truth of God publicly two or three times each week. That is a cruel, wasteful, and impractical order. The church's first business is with the truth, not with machinery, even the most sanctified ecclesiastical machinery. And yet it happens often that the only interest of a church court in a young minister is whether or not his church is raising its budget and is receiving a substantial number of new members. Whether or not he knows what the Christian gospel is and is able to preach and teach it effectively in his parish is not considered a fit subject for inquiry.

There seem to be two attitudes to this matter that are widely prevalent. The first is that a man's doctrine is a purely private concern between him and his God and that he must be permitted to go his own way without interference from any quarter, an attitude that encourages the most unrestrained individualism and makes it impossible for the church as a whole to be a responsible confessional church. The second attitude is the exact opposite, where some one minister or group of ministers professes to have arrived at the perfection of Christian doctrine and feels competent, therefore, to pronounce unerring judgments on the doctrine of all fellow ministers, an arrogance and presumption that is equally destructive of theological health in the church. There is, however, a third possibility that is the responsibly Christian attitude: to recognize that no question is more important in the life of the church than the integrity of the gospel we preach and of the principles upon which we act as a church; that this is an area in which none of us has any reason for arrogance, since, if we know our own hearts, we know that there is sin and error both in us and in our doctrine and that we need constantly to be delivered out of error into truth; and finally that all of us without exception need the fellowship and assistance of other ministers in the struggle against error and in the search for truth.

The most serious blindness in us is always below the level of our consciousness and most difficult for us to recognize. The greatest weaknesses in our ministries are ones in which we are encouraged by our congregations. The worst prejudices to which we are subject are those which we share with our communities and therefore are in danger of considering to be points of unusual wisdom in ourselves. Therefore, we are in constant need of being exposed to a theological critique that will probe the weak points in our doctrinal armor, force us to a reconsideration of our established principles, and keep us asking ourselves whether or not what we are saying and doing is what we should be saying and doing as faithful ministers of the Jesus Christ who was crucified on Calvary. To be a theologian is not, first and foremost, to have at our command all the theological learning of the ages; it is, rather, that part of our ministry in which we deliberately expose ourselves, our church, our preaching, to ruthless searching criticism, first in the light of the Scriptures and then in the light of what the church has said and done across the ages, that we may with greater confidence and integrity speak and act in days yet to come. To be a theologian is simply to take the question of Christian truth with complete seriousness, acknowledging that we are responsible to God not only for sins in our conduct but also for untruth in our doctrine. We cannot withhold the seemingly harsh judgment, then, that a minister who does not in any way do the work of a theologian is a minister who does not take seriously the problem of error in his own gospel and in the life of the church.

A minister, if he is sensitive to the responsibility of his office, early finds himself in a painful dilemma. He has a passionate devotion to Jesus Christ and a desire to preach his gospel with purity and power. He chooses subjects that seem to him to be of urgent importance and prepares sermons on them. Each sermon is a proclamation of Christian truth. But after a time he begins to be uncomfortably aware of tensions and even contradictions in his preaching. The truth that was declared with all earnestness on March 15 does not seem to fit together too well with the truth that was declared with equal earnestness one Sunday in the preceding November. Then perhaps the question arises in the mind as to how these particular convictions concerning the truth became a part of his gospel. Some came from his home life and training, some from ministers and church school teachers, some from theological teachers and theological books, some from schoolmates, some from the atmosphere of the age. How, then, can he be sure whether or not they are true? An idea is not necessarily true because someone we respect has held it to be true and now we hold it and are enthusiastic about it. In the past, earnest people have been enthusiastic about false gospels. A doctrine can appeal to people not because it is true but because it enables them to evade the truth. There must be some criterion to which a man can appeal in this dilemma if he is not to become lost in a hopeless sea of relativity and become content to say, "At least this is true for me." The problem is even more acute if he becomes aware that a minister, like everyone else, is inevitably a child of his time, shaped in mind and spirit by all the influences of the world around him, and sharing the peculiar sins and blindnesses of his age. How, then, can he stand next Sunday in his pulpit and declare with confidence what is the very truth of God for his people?

It is this predicament in which all of us are involved that drives us to work at theology, not as a side line of the ministry, but as the only way of escape from its most painful dilemma. Theology is the careful systematic investigation of the problem of truth and error in the church's message and principles. Our constant dilemma between truth and error sends us first of all to the Scriptures as to the one place where light, the light of God, shines into our darkness and reveals to us the otherwise hidden line between truth and falsehood, between a true church and a false church, between a true faith and attractive but false substitutes for faith. The prophets and the apostles have the eyes of faith, what Barth calls "the cat's eyes that see in the dark," by which they see what we in our blindness have been unable to see, and they lend us their eyes that we may cease to be blind in our present situation. In too much of our theologizing, the Scriptures occupy a secondary rather than a primary place. We are tempted to go directly to what seem to us to be the wisest and soundest interpreters of theological principles (and every denomination and every group within each denomination has its select theologians to whom it looks for guidance) as though we could take over a sound theology from them. One man looks to Luther, another to Calvin, another to Schleiermacher, another to Barth, another to Bultmann. It is this which brings confusion and division in the church. We should have learned from Paul in I Corinthians that theological interpreters, even though their names be Peter and Paul and Apollos, bring confusion and division in the church unless first we have our ears opened to hear *for ourselves* the word of the gospel to which all faithful interpreters merely bear witness. Paul does not point to Paul, nor Peter to Peter, nor Luther to Luther, nor Calvin to Calvin; each points beyond himself to a word and deed of God in Jesus Christ that every man has to hear for himself and know that it has been done for him. We go first to the Scriptures, then, as the place where we may have our eyes opened to the revelation of God and to the saving work of God in the midst of men, a revelation and a work that are so infinitely far beyond all weak human apprehensions and interpretations of it that we can never rest completely satisfied for long in any theological formulation of it, our own or anyone else's — and only then are we able to profit from the writings of even the greatest theologians. It is from the Scriptures and from them alone that we get our criterion of truth, not in any abstract sense, but as the knowledge of the true God and of what it means to be a true man and what is the nature of a true church and what is the true destiny not only of humanity in general but also of each one of us.

Many ministers and theological students experience the difficulty of the man who complained that his theology at any particular moment was that of the book that he had last read or of the theologian whom he had last heard. Each of them wrote or spoke so convincingly, and seemed to him so genuinely Christian, that he was certain what each one said must be true. And yet he was aware that they represented very different and even contradictory theologies. Therefore, he had come to feel that he himself was a kind of theological chameleon merely reflecting the varying colors of the theological spectrum. That is the situation of a man who has no criterion. He is unable to think for himself, so that he is constantly relaying secondhand thoughts about the gospel. Only too often that is the plight of the Christian preacher and teacher in America today. There is no adequate remedy for it until the minister becomes seriously a theologian whose first theological task is the investigation of the Scriptures, not just to find texts for future sermons, but to let them speak their own truth in their own way, no matter how upsetting it may be to his preconceived ideas or to the religious preconceptions of the members of his congregation.

If the truth were told, many ministers find the investigation of Scripture a rather boring occupation, and they do not use Scripture much in preaching because they are doubtful of their ability to make it interesting to their congregations. This is so because the Bible is still for them merely a book of religion and morality that never tells them anything essentially that they do not already know. But let them wrestle with it until in its pages the same God meets them and speaks with them who met and spoke with Amos and Isaiah and Peter and Paul and calls them to take up in our day the same task that rested upon prophets and apostles, and there will no longer be anything boring about the investigation of Scripture. Rather, each new confrontation with Scripture will be a new confrontation with the living God in which we begin to be aware of the mind of God concerning ourselves and our people and our world. Then and only then do we have a criterion and guide in our search for truth, but not as a theological yardstick with which we can readily determine the truth or falsehood of different theologies, for our criterion and guide is the living God himself, the God of truth, who alone is able to lead his church into all truth, and who is present with us in his Word only as we are willing to receive him in humility and faith. The Scriptures are primary in our theologizing because it is through them alone that we have the firsthand knowledge of God which is fellowship with him and with our brothers in the truth (I John 1:3).

It is not sufficient, however, that we search the Scriptures each of us alone. Our very approach to them is conditioned by the fact that we are members of a church that has been interpreting the Scriptures for centuries and whose course and character of life has been determined by what it has found or has failed to find in them. The history of the church has been in a very real sense the history of its dialogue with Scripture, that is, with the God whom it knows through the Scriptures. Or perhaps we should put it in this way: that the primary commentary on the meaning of Scripture is that which has been written by the Holy Spirit in the life of the church. For instance, when we want to understand what Paul means by his statement that we are justified not by works but by faith, we read, not only Romans and Galatians and the relevant passages in the Gospels, but also the history of theology and of the church in the sixteenth century where we see laid out before us two churches, one built on a nicely balanced doctrine of salvation by faith-combined-with-various-religious-works and the other built upon a radical doctrine of salvation by faith alone. It is presumptuous for any minister to think he can go directly from the word of Scripture to the situation of the present day without taking into account the earnest wrestling of the church across the ages with the meaning of the Scriptures for life. That is the surest way of making all the mistakes over again that Christians have made in the past. It is also an evidence of blindness to what God the Holy Spirit has been doing in the church through the centuries, which is usually accompanied by a blindness to what God the Holy Spirit is doing in the church now. We must acknowledge, therefore, that we cannot and dare not stand alone as interpreters of Scripture. We stand, rather, as the representatives in the present day of a vast company of preachers and scholars who have spent their lives in spelling out the truth of God according to the Scriptures, and in their books they make available to us what they have learned. We are under no compulsion to agree with them, no matter how venerable they may be, for even the most venerable of them were imperfect in their understanding, but we are under obligation to hear them and to learn from them whatever they can teach us so that more and more our interpretation may lose its individualistic superficiality and may take on the breadth and depth of an understanding that is the possession of the church universal. The great theologians of the various ages of the church have done their thinking on *our* behalf concerning *our* problems of interpretation. They wrote their books for us that we might be kept from falsifying the gospel in the twentieth century. And for us to attempt to do the work of the ministry without any serious study of their works is to profess that we do not need them as our teachers. In fact, the neglect of theology by a minister has always implicit in it the egotistical assumption that he has such a mastery of the truth of the gospel that he does not need to be a student any longer, sitting at the feet of the great teachers that God has from time to time given to his church.

There are many other reasons why a minister should be a theologian, but there is space to mention only one or two. He should be aware that we begin to know what our own convictions are only when we listen carefully to other men saying what they believe and why. There is no better exercise for the clarification of our own faith than to choose some theologian whose ability commands our respect but with whom we are not conscious of any close agreement and to study a number of his books with care until he has become an intimate companion whose thinking we must take with complete seriousness. If he is a theologian of real stature, he will make us rethink our own theological positions, and before we are finished with him we shall know that we have been through an inner battle in which our faith has been clarified and strengthened. Theological thinking is a social experience; it cannot be done by any one man in isolation. We may be isolated physically, but through the medium of books we must be in dialogue with other minds if there is to be any vitality in our thinking. This is why it is fatal to the quality of our ministries if we read only popular religious literature, inspirational books as they are called. They merely stimulate us to go on thinking in pretty much the same channels with which we are already familiar. The great works of theology pull us out of the accustomed grooves and make us struggle with thoughts that are unfamiliar. They raise the central issues of Christian life and thought in ever-new forms and present to our minds a consistent solution of those issues which by its consistency makes us aware of our inconsistencies and by its thoroughness makes us aware of the brokenness and incompleteness of our answers.

It is also part of our theological task to be constantly studying the man of our time to whom we proclaim the gospel. The word of God is always a word to a particular man in a particular situation. It is never truth in general that can be abstracted from all historical particularities. For this reason, sermons that are the result of studying the Scriptures alone, or the Scriptures and some theology of the past, are likely to be barren and profitless no matter how earnest the work that is put into them. Jesus' words have in them the eternal truth of God, but they have also in them a profound understanding of the people to whom they are addressed. We must be students of the life of our day, not content with superficial impressions of it but studying it in all its manifestations, that we may speak with understanding to the man of our time. There is a very great danger to which we are exposed as ministers that we may let ourselves be closed off from the real world into an artificial religious world in which no one speaks or acts quite as they do in the real world. It is only too true that people adjust not only their language but also their behavior and the tenor of their thoughts when they see us coming. Therefore, if we read only the surface of life, we are not likely to understand our people at the level of their real existence. Added to this is the fact that often they are extremely confused about themselves: they are not what they think they are. Their most serious problems are not the ones of which they are most conscious. We must therefore use every possible means of penetrating the surface of life and getting at the real problems. This understanding of the man to whom we speak is part of our theological problem. Light upon it will come to us from the Scriptures and from theological literature but also from the study of all the manifestations of man's life today. Nothing is alien to our study that is important to the life of man. And here again we must call attention to the presumption of the minister who thinks he knows who the man is to whom he is addressing his message and feels under no necessity to undertake any careful critical study of the matter. Only the man who confesses himself baffled again and again before the mystery of the man of our time and who therefore follows every possible clue to gain a deeper understanding of him is likely to penetrate the surface level of life and speak a word that goes anywhere near the roots of man's problems. The minister stands between two mysteries — the mystery of God and the mystery of man. If his eyes are open, then he knows what a short distance he has penetrated into both mysteries and he is preserved from any possibility of glibness or cocksureness in his speaking. The function of his theology is to keep his eyes ever open to the magnitude of the mysteries with which he dares to deal and to make him content if week by week and day by day he can find a few words that he can speak with honesty, some as words from God to man, some as words on man's behalf to God.

The Problem of Time

There is still a problem about the place of theology in the minister's pattern of life. Theology is essential to his ministry, and its neglect has at every point serious consequences for the character of his work. But he is likely to regard it as an extra burden that is being loaded upon his back, one for which in his busy life it seems impossible that he should ever find time. The busyness of the American minister is one of his chief problems and one of the chief obstacles to the wholeness and effectiveness of his ministry. We may have a multitude of things to do, but if we become busy, we are lost.

It is curious how many people are under the impression that they have no time for things that are essential to life itself. It is a sickness of our American society with serious consequences for church life, family life, and for the individuals themselves. But what hope is there for its diagnosis or cure if the physician himself has the disease? We have all the time there is, all and more than all that most men in earlier centuries have had. Few of us have as little time in our ministries as Jesus had — and yet he did all that he had to do. It is not the quantity of time that matters but what goes on in the time we have. Therefore, the primary question concerning theological study, or pastoral work, or the careful preparation of sermons, or the training of adult leaders, is not, How can we find time for it? but rather, Can we be faithful in the ministry of Jesus Christ without finding time for it? We always find time for whatever we consider essential to our existence. It is not an exaggeration to say that theology, properly understood, is as essential to the existence of a minister as food and sleep are to the existence of our bodies.

There is little likelihood, however, of any minister's sustaining regular and intensive theological studies unless he has the sympathy, support, and co-operation of his congregation in this as in all other departments of his work. The point should be made very clear that theological study in the ministry is not a private interest, a personal hobby; it is one very important part of the total ministry that we undertake in the service of the church. We study our theology for the sake of our congregations, that we may have the knowledge and understanding that are essential in every aspect of the life of the church. We are servants of the Word before we are servants of our congregations, and we can serve our people effectively only when we have given our hearts and minds devotedly to the study in Scriptures, theology, history, and life, of that Word which is the bread of life.

Ministers sometimes speak of " stealing " time from congregational duties for theological study. They are not aware of serving their people when they are studying in the same degree as when they are making a sick call. They shrink from setting apart hours for undisturbed study for fear they will be thought to be neglecting more urgent duties. This problem exists because of the failure of ministers to give their congregations a proper understanding of what is involved in the work of the ministry. Many of the members of the church see the minister only on a Sunday morning or on formal occasions and have no idea whatsoever of how he spends his time. Thus it is easy for them to have the idea that he should be available to them at any moment whether or not their concern is an urgent one, and they may thoughtlessly involve him in time-consuming activities in the community that should be left for someone else. If they are to respect their minister's time and his need to set a strict order upon it, then they must be given some understanding of the magnitude and complexity and strenuousness of the tasks that are involved in the ministry. The nature of the ministry is a subject on which every minister should preach from time to time, not just that his members may understand his task, but that they may better understand the nature of the church of which they are a part and may begin to see that they too are called as Christians to have a ministry. Far too rarely do we invite them to share our ministry with us at least in some degree. Perhaps the secret of finding time for theology is to broaden the scope of the ministry within the congregation and to enlist and train members of the congregation to discharge many of the duties and functions that at present fall to the minister alone.

7

EVANGELISM

The Mission at Our Very Door

A YOUNG minister, ten years in a new suburban church and more than a little proud of his seven hundred members, had just one complaint: "Because they started as a mission, my people, in spite of everything I say, go on thinking of our church as a mission." Gently it had to be suggested to him that he was leading them blindly in the wrong direction. The sheep were wiser than the shepherd. The vital problem in most churches is to get the members to think of their church as a mission and themselves as missionaries. To most people in the churches of America their church is a venerable religious institution offering an opportunity for worship for all who care to attend and a complex of organizations to nourish the lives of members and provide opportunities for service. It supports missions in underprivileged sections of America and in lands across the seas, but to suggest that it should be a mission to people beyond its doors in its own community is likely only to make many members (and perhaps also the minister) uncomfortable.

It is traditional in most churches to have missionary societies in which persons, mainly women, meet regularly to study missions and to raise money for their support. The missions studied and supported are usually at a distance. Rarely does such a society interest itself in any local project that would require its members to engage actively in a mission to people close at hand. And yet it requires little investigation to discover that in our towns and cities nearly half the population lives outside the bounds of any religious fellowship and the community has in it a great many people, who, while they reckon themselves officially as belonging to some denomination because of a contact in the past, are actually cut off from any church and cannot of themselves find the way back, even though they need desperately the faith and understanding and fellowship the church should make available to them. When a person who has grown up in the church leaves the church for some reason and ten or fifteen years pass without his returning, it becomes very difficult for him to walk in a church door and down the aisle to a seat. If the reason for leaving was disillusionment with the church or some serious doubt, the person may go on for years with a false conception of both the church and the Christian faith, with no one to show him anything different. Then there are the thousands who have grown up outside the church entirely, have been wrestling for years with the problems of their lives without the benefit of any of the understanding that is the gift of faith, and have never in all their contacts with Christians learned anything that would draw them toward the church. Outside each church door is a field for missions, often a vast field, but strangely many of our churches are neither conscious of the call to mission close at hand nor equipped in their membership to take advantage of the opportunity.

At a dinner for church school teachers in a large city congregation that had seven hundred children in its church school, the superintendent began describing to me how much more difficult his work was than it ought to be because of the fact that half the children came from families of which the adults had no connection with the church, contributed nothing to the church, and merely shelved the responsibility for their children's religious training onto the church school. Inquiry drew forth the information that neither teachers, church officers, nor ministers had ever visited these families to get acquainted with them, to invite them to church, or to find why they held aloof from the church. The sending of the children showed at least a vestige of religious concern. The families of the three hundred and fifty children offered a magnificent opportunity for Christian outreach, but this particular church had no eyes to see.

Jesus found the people outside the synagogue more interesting and more responsive to him than those on the inside who had grown up in faithful participation in its worship and were ostensibly the godly people of the community. The publicans and sinners were more honest about their needs than the regular synagogue attenders who found it difficult to acknowledge that there was anything wrong between them and God that needed to be set right. But many a minister goes on for years faithfully ministering to his flock and to such newcomers as find their way into his church and make themselves known to him, before he breaks out as Jesus did over the wall of the religious community to make contact with outsiders. Some never break out and so miss entirely the joy of ministering where the need is greatest and the response, both positive and negative, refreshing in its honesty and simplicity.

My work was interrupted one morning by a man whose shabby clothing and bleary eyes, plus a faint odor of whisky, made me anticipate a plea for money to be used for more whisky. To my surprise he asked instead if he could go into the church. He stood first at the chancel steps, looking at a beautiful stained-glass window, and his words, when he spoke, had in them a quite surprising appreciation of the beauty. He had had little contact with any church for more than twenty years. The story came out little by little during later visits. He was pensioned from his work because of chronic sickness. He was an alcoholic but was trying to get the better of it. He had been a Communist and an atheist for half his life. The Party had given him a free trip to Russia. He was widely read in history, philosophy, and general literature and spent much of his time in reading. In the preceding year his wife had died and his son had had to cross the continent to live with an aunt. That very week he had in his loneliness sought out old companions, and one drink had led to another until all his month's allowance for food was gone. But his turning in at the church door was in hope of more than food. The only Christians who in the past had tried to do anything for him were members of a small evangelistic church that he was persuaded to attend several times but whose hearty worship and naïve theology had left him cold. He was hungry to know what there was for him in the Christian gospel. Sick of communism, sick of atheism, and facing dark, lonely days in isolation, with only a sense of emptiness within in spite of his joy in books, there were, nevertheless, no quick ready-made solutions for him; he had to find his way back step by step. The reason for telling the story is twofold. This man symbolizes the outsider of our time in his unbelief, unhappy in it, alienated from the church, not to be reached by any sentimental type of evangelism, waiting at the very threshold of the church to be discovered. (He had been living for a year in a garret not a hundred yards from the church, with church members nearby, but no one had known of his existence.) But, more important, he warns us that a church that undertakes to reach such thoughtful unbelievers needs representatives who are as serious in their thinking about life's meaning as the unbeliever is.

The Revival of Interest in Evangelism

There has been a revival of interest in evangelism in recent years. It seems to have been stimulated in a number of different ways and behind some of them at least we would see the working of the Spirit of God. First, there has been an awakening among Christians to the existence of a world of unbelief at their door. They had grown accustomed to thinking of their world as a Christian world in antithesis to the non-Christian world in Asia and Africa. It was customary to speak of European and North American countries as "Christian countries." The term "Christendom" was a familiar one at Christian conferences and in Christian writing; it signified the realm beyond the church that had been leavened with Christian influences and so could be designated as Christian, even though a profession of the Christian faith might be lacking. Christians, impressed by the slight distinction between people inside the church and people outside the church but within Christendom, came to the conclusion that evangelization had little point. In fact, it was a sign of one's lack of proper respect for informal Christians. Since 1933, however, there has been less and less talk of Christendom. We have learned that the docile world outside the church may cease to be docile and to let itself be called semi-Christian and may suddenly crystalize into forms that threaten the very existence of the church. It has happened in one country after another, and many of our sister churches are living today in communities that are unfriendly to the profession and practice of the Christian faith. It is amazing in the light of what has happened in countries of Eastern Europe that were traditionally Christian for centuries, that in Britain and North America members of the churches are still on the whole undisturbed and largely unconcerned about the non-Christian world in which they have their daily existence.

A second source of renewed interest in evangelism has been statistical. A number of old established denominations suddenly became aware that in a swiftly growing nation their own membership had been remarkably static for many years. They had been receiving only sufficient new members to replace those who were dying or dropping out. And yet in the same period other newer churches had multiplied their membership many times over. Not all were equally disturbed by this condition. One distinguished churchman, commenting on it in a church magazine, made a memorable remark. He gave statistics concerning the rapid growth of what he called " store-front churches " and their remarkable success in reaching the masses. And then, at the point where one expected an appeal for a new outlook and attitude by his own church, he wrote: " Our church has been traditionally a church of the middle and upper classes in society. Therefore, let us give our blessing to the store-front churches in their mission to the masses while we continue our mission to the classes." " After all," says the comfortable churchman, " those people wouldn't be very happy in our kind of church." It does not occur to him that Jesus Christ himself might not be very happy in his kind of church! But neither in secular nor in sacred organizations do we like to be open to the accusation that we are stagnant, that we are only holding our own and not moving ahead, so that the appeal to statistics makes us at least susceptible to evangelism.

A third source of interest has been historical and theological. There has been a rediscovery of the church and of what the church has been in history. In its beginnings it was not an institution but rather a mission, a bold and seemingly fantastic mission as a little group of Jews set out to claim the whole world for their Lord, Jesus Christ. Whenever it has ceased to be a mission and has become content to be merely a religious institution, it has withered and died. But again and again it has happened that out of the dry shell a new missionary impulse has broken forth with important consequences for the world. Therefore, in the light of history a church that is not a mission invading the world has reason to suspect that, however successful and impressive it is outwardly, it is in the throes of death.

A fourth, and certainly the chief source of all, has been the revolution in Biblical understanding to which reference has already been made. The Bible has been coming open in men's hands in the midst of world revolutions. With old securities snatched away, men have been given ears to hear in the Scriptures a word that penetrates to the depth of their situation. They no longer laugh at the claim that there is a word from God that is the answer to man's critical dilemmas. They are more ready than they have been in a long time to set a question mark not against the Christian word but against their own assured ideas. Principles that have been assumed as self-evident by Western man have been shaken by the events of the mid-twentieth century. The Bible has been coming open, and we have been hearing in it a gospel that has been hidden even from the church, so that ministers and laymen alike have to let it be spelled out for them as though they had never heard it before. The old familiar words " salvation," " grace," "justification," " faith," " Spirit," words that we heard and spoke hundreds of times, suddenly have a mean-

ing in them of which we never dreamed. Jesus Christ throws
off the graveclothes with which we bound him and comes forth
from his twentieth-century tomb to vindicate his word as the
word of truth and his Spirit as the Spirit of power that, when
it speaks through his word in a man's heart and life, takes possession of him for God. It is a combination of forces, then, that
has created a situation in the church that at least points toward
a rebirth of evangelizing power.

The interest in evangelism has resulted in two forms of activity, mass evangelism and visitation evangelism, the former a
return to the traditional evangelistic techniques of an earlier
generation with the use of modern methods of advertising and
organization, and the latter a newly devised plan for the invasion
of the community by trained teams of lay visitors. The question
that must be asked concerning both is whether they succeed in
reaching beyond the church community to the world outside.
A church that has been remarkably unsuccessful in reaching the
world of unbelievers beyond its walls dare not be too critical of
any endeavor that in any measure succeeds in doing that very
thing. The chief criticism of mass evangelism in its modern form
is that such a high percentage of its attenders and converts are
young people and adults who are already within the church and
are sensitive to the appeal to dedicate themselves more fully to
Christ than they have in the past. Unfortunately the rededication
sometimes takes them out of the church to which they belonged
and attaches them to a more evangelistic form of church. Also,
mass evangelism has a strong tendency to attach itself firmly to
a literalistic interpretation of the Bible that alienates many
thoughtful inquirers, and to a theology that does not take with
sufficient seriousness the Biblical truth that the salvation of the
soul is the salvation of the whole man in his personal, social,
economic, and political existence. It is not unfair to say that it
has been much more successful in strengthening the fundamen-
talist movement within the churches than in making any deep
impression upon the non-Christian world beyond all our churches.

Visitation evangelism has in many ways been more effective

than mass evangelism. It requires the training of laymen in the local church to prepare them to make visits in homes and to engage in conversations concerning the Christian faith, and it gives these laymen a taste of what it means to approach others in the name of Jesus Christ. It is therefore a venture in evangelism by the local church and not merely by a professional team on behalf of the local church and with its co-operation, so that it is likely to have a profounder effect in reshaping the mind and interest of the local church. Also, it is a movement that sends members of the church in search of persons and families that are outside the fellowship of the church, and it has brought far more new members into the church than mass evangelism has. Its weakness is its tendency to degenerate in some instances into a membership campaign that is more interested in adding people to the roll of the church than in engaging in genuine Christian conversation with persons who are outside the Christian faith. We ought not to rejoice that it is so easy to persuade people to join the church; it indicates only that they have no comprehension of what they are doing; they would join any socially approved club if invited with the same enthusiasm and warmth and without any more severe demands upon them.

The rivalry of churches in their eagerness for external growth can have serious consequences for both church and ministry. A congregation falls under the delusion that numbers constitute strength and that increase in numbers indicates vitality and authenticity. It is a truly Christian church because, if it were not, it would not be so vigorous in growth. The suggestion then is that congregations that are not growing in the same manner have something wrong with them and their ministers are seriously defective in some way. This emphasis upon growth leads easily to a lowering of standards, so that people are swept into the membership of the church without any adequate preparation for it, without any clear confrontation with the claims of the gospel and so without any real decision of faith. The apology for this procedure is sometimes made that now at least they are within the circle of the church and the church has the opportunity of reaching them with its gospel. But when they find so many already inside the church who know little more of what it all means than they do, are they likely to take seriously their need for anything more? The consequence for the church is serious, for the success in numbers, if it be of this character, only increases the confusion of faith within the church itself. The effect upon the ministry is equally serious. A minister comes to be judged according to his ability to secure new members and not by the quality of his total ministry. Vacancy committees get into the habit of choosing their candidates by running the eye down the column in the last three years' reports for their denomination in which the number of new members received is reported, with a glance perhaps at the column that indicates increase in funds raised. The result is an unhealthy and sometimes almost frantic urgency, on the part of ministers, about membership campaigns and fund-raising with a corresponding decline of interest in serious Biblical and theological discussions that might help them toward a more truly evangelical ministry.

The Basic Problem

It must now be said of both visitation and mass evangelism that they arise from the church's consciousness of its failure to reach the world at its door, that they are attempts to break through the barrier that divides the church from the world, but that neither has a sufficiently clear discernment of what it is in the church that forms that barrier. Neither goes deep enough in diagnosing the sickness of the church. Not that it is a hidden sickness, for its manifestations are everywhere in the life of the church once one has eyes to see them. That is the very problem. The sickness has become so universal that it is accepted as an inevitable characteristic of normal church life. It is like stealing in Sparta where the practice was so universal that no one was conscious of anything wrong with it. With rare exceptions we have become a nonevangelizing church (and this is true even of some rapidly growing churches), a church in which we can converse with each other as long as certain basic Christian assumptions are made by all of us but in which we have lost the capacity of conversing with persons for whom all Christian or religious assumptions are set in question. Confronted with unbelief, we become incoherent. This is the acute embarrassment of many Christian parents with their children. The child is so often the simple naïve expression of honest human unbelief. The child has not yet learned to dissemble concerning the questions that existence thrusts upward in his mind. But to the parent the questions are distressing and embarrassing because they expose to him his incapacity as a representative of the Christian faith to deal with unbelief in all its stark reality. They are members of a non-evangelizing church because the Christian faith as they know it is a nonevangelizing faith. Their kind of Christianity has never concerned itself with the problem of how an unbeliever through the ministry of a believer may pass from unbelief to faith. Therefore, even with their own children they are helpless to point any way out of unbelief. If their best friend were to confess himself to them as utterly cut off from God and forced in honesty to say that the whole Christian faith was incredible to him, they would be in dire straits to know what to do. Their life in the church and their education in the Christian faith has not equipped them to be useful and coherent in that situation.

It is this incoherence of the ordinary Christian which is the clue to the problem. He may be quite coherent on a hundred other subjects and even in the discussion of religious matters in general but completely speechless when confronted with a situation in which he has to speak as a believing Christian to an unbelieving world. But the layman is not alone in his speechlessness. Frequently the man in the pulpit is afflicted with the same speechlessness when faced not with " good Christians " who seem to need only improvement and strengthening in their faith but with intelligent, conscientious unbelievers who say, " We do not believe, not because we do not want to believe, but because in honesty we are unable to consent to the truth of the central Christian affirmations." Suddenly the minister, in spite of all his years of thought and study, is shaken into an awareness of how much of his faith he himself has taken for granted in the protected atmosphere of the Christian fellowship.

This problem of incoherence in the face of unbelief becomes singularly acute in an era such as the present when in one country after another the armistice of polite relations between church and world is coming to an end. The mask of politeness is being cast aside by unbelief, so that the church is forced to take account of the radical antithesis between believing and not believing. It is no mark of wisdom or discernment for Christians to be shocked that the world should assert itself as a world that denies and even hates the church and gospel. There are sufficient warnings for them in Scripture concerning the nature of the world. Both in the Old and in the New Testament the world stubbornly resists the claim made upon it by the word of God. At the cross the world, through the agency of venerable religious and political authorities, tries once and for all to silence the word in which God undercuts all human securities and sets the whole of man's life radically in question. It was a delusion for men to think that the world in its old age was so tamed by religion and philosophy that it could mean no harm. It is therefore to be welcomed that at last we are being shocked out of our delusions and forced to recognize the magnitude of the problems with which we as a church and ministry are confronted in the world of our time. In an era in which unbelief has suddenly found its tongue and speaks with persuasive power and bold assurance, a church that remains incoherent has no future.

One of the most hopeful signs in the present-day church is that it is distressed by this problem. It will be unfortunate if this distress is relieved by the participation of churches in mass evangelism campaigns. It is much easier to co-operate in a series of meetings or in a program of visitation than to submit oneself to the long discipline by which alone the understanding and the faith come to fruition that are necessary for effective evangelical witness. In short, it is easier to engage in certain new activities than to become a different kind of Christian and a different kind of church. The danger therefore is that, after participation in mass and visitation evangelism, the Christian congregation may be the same nonevangelizing church that it was before because the depth of the problem has been neither recognized nor considered, but now it is a church with a good conscience because it has participated in a project in evangelism.

One aspect of the problem is that many Christians are speechless in matters that concern their faith in reaction against the glibness of evangelicals whose specialty is to approach boldly not only unbelievers but all persons who have not had the same kind of experience that they have had or do not hold the same doctrines that they hold. Their zeal to make converts may well put our established churches to shame. Their boldness of approach makes us embarrassingly conscious of our own timidity. But the flood of pious phraseology that pours from them each time they speak, and their evident claim to have the answers ready-made for all questions, makes us, and many others with us, anxious to escape from them at the earliest opportunity. Often hidden behind their words is a simplicity and earnestness of faith, but the faith is imprisoned by the phrases, like a human face hiding behind a mask. The phrases make real conversation impossible, since they are to such a degree a formalized religious expression, and, since they are held to be the absolute truth, they never vary in any situation. The individual is relieved of the painful necessity of finding for himself the words that are an honest witness to his faith, just as the communist is relieved by the book phrases of his political and economic creed from the burden of thinking for himself concerning the realities of the problem before he speaks. The artificiality of religious speech of this kind accounts for the unease we may feel at its stifling of genuine Christian conversation between persons. Its revival is not likely to help us in the evangelization of the sophisticated and often highly intelligent world of unbelief that confronts us. It is more likely to complicate the situation and to be an obstructing factor in real communication. What must be found is language in which Christians can speak to one another and to non-Christians in the simplest and most unsentimental and realistic way concerning the faith and the life that are theirs in and through Jesus Christ; that is, in a way that corresponds to the realities.

EVANGELISM IN THE NEW TESTAMENT

Evangelism in the New Testament is no secondary problem, since Christians then and for a long time to come were acutely aware of themselves as a tiny island of faith in a vast sea of unbelief. When the world turned on them and threatened them with destruction, a future for them seemed possible only by a miracle. They had no basis for complacency. But what is most striking in the early church is that evangelism seems not to have been something that was organized but rather an exuberant and irresistible overflow of faith and life and joy in God. There was something in the nature of the existence of the ordinary Christian that made him inevitably a channel of communication for the gospel to the world of unbelief.

Judaism drew a sharp line and built a high barrier between the world of belief and the world of unbelief. It was much easier to slip over the line or through the barrier into the world outside the religious community than to make one's way back in again. Undoubtedly there were some Jews who made the journey back, and there were Gentiles who became either baptized and circumcised converts, or else "God-fearers," less firmly attached to the synagogue. But Judaism was essentially a nonevangelizing religious community. It was deeply concerned about the preservation of a pure religious tradition. It maintained the inerrancy of its Scriptures. It was severe in the extreme in insisting upon high moral standards. It provided for orderly worship and encouraged charity. But its attitude to unbelievers was chiefly one of repulsion and avoidance. In antithesis to this, Jesus considered himself " sent to the lost sheep of the house of Israel." The outsiders were increasingly his major concern. He calls them " the sick " who have the primary claim upon the physician's time. The source of his evangelism is thus his compassion for men in their sickness and his longing to restore them to the wholeness of their life in God. Perhaps we can go one stage farther back and find the source of this compassion and longing in the wholeness of his own life in God, the joy that was his in that perfect wholeness, and the consciousness of a compulsion in the joy itself that he should share it with every sick and broken specimen of humanity. Jesus Christ could not possess his own life in God without giving the life that was his in God to others. He did not achieve this giving by merely speaking words to them. Words had to be spoken, not always words that were specially marked as religious words, but before and in and after his speaking he had to give himself. There was no evangelism without self-giving. Perhaps that is one reason why the process was so painfully slow. Jesus did not sweep masses of people into his movement. He seems rather to have made disciples one by one and to have been unconcerned about numbers. There was also an urgency in his mission, not just because the time was short but because of his eagerness to reach the poor, the broken, the prisoners, the blind.

In the early church as we see it in The Acts there is the same slow but steady growth. The thousands who were added to the church at Pentecost ought not to be quoted as a validation of mass evangelism since they were most likely the sudden harvest of seed sown by Jesus during his ministry. People did not rush into a church that was branded as a dangerously revolutionary movement, that warned each convert that he must be ready to suffer for his faith, and that expected of him an uncompromising faithfulness to God. Jesus had set the disciples an example of not encouraging anyone to make a beginning in the life of discipleship unless he was ready to go all the way through with it regardless of the cost. Salvation was free in the sense that it was the gift of God, but it was also costly to the believer.

It is essential to any understanding of the early church that we grasp what is signified by the receiving of the Holy Spirit, which, according to Acts, ch. 2, empowered the church for its ministry. John the Baptist's anticipation concerning Jesus was that he would baptize men with the Holy Spirit, that is, that he would set God as a living presence within their hearts. The ministry of Jesus is everywhere in the Gospels interpreted as a ministry in the power of the Spirit. He preaches and heals and liberates men from evil powers with a strange unearthly power because of his oneness with God. His forgiveness is God's forgiveness because his love is God's love. So one with God is he that his humanity is the perfect reflection of God's nature. It was this Spirit of God who dwelt in all his fullness in him that he sought to impart to his disciples. That he succeeded in some measure is evidenced by the power of their ministry, but always in them there was stubborn resistance. We are not fair to them unless we imaginatively grasp what it must have meant to be the first of all humanity to have the claim made upon them that they must die unto self in order to live unto God. The self in man does not die easily, even in intimate fellowship with one such as Jesus. But the cross, and the resurrection that unveiled the cross's meaning to them, shattered their self-centeredness and laid them unconditionally open to God. The cross made them ready for Pentecost.

The Spirit, who took possession of Christians at Pentecost, was, then, not just a vague spiritual influence or presence, but the Spirit of Jesus Christ empowering them for the same ministry that was his. They tasted the same wholeness, oneness with God, and unconquerable joy, yet not the same, since in them as long as life lasted there would be a residue of resistance to the Spirit. They were men and not God. But they were men upon whom God had poured out such riches of the Spirit and compassed with such love that they were compelled from within to use any and every opportunity that offered to communicate something of their faith and life to others. That a man was an unbeliever meant to them simply that he was a man in desperate need of what they had to give, whether he knew it or not. No one had to tell them that they ought to evangelize. The very life that was God's gift to them in Christ had in its intrinsic universality the imperative of evangelism. It was by its nature the true life of every man, and until they learned of it and came to possess it, men would be forced to live bereft of their true selves. To offer it to other men was not to offer them something alien to them, a foreign religion, a Hebrew code of morals; it was to offer them the life that had been intended for them by their Creator from the beginning. Evangelism thus was not something added, but rather it belonged to the essence of the faith that possessed the early Christians, so that to be a Christian was to be entrusted with a treasure that grew in richness the more widely it was shared.

THE PARALYZING MYTH OF THE " GOOD CHRISTIAN "

Perhaps now we shall be able to delve below the surface of that incoherence and speechlessness of the Christian confronted with honest unbelief that makes the church a nonevangelizing church. But let us be careful. We shall only make him more incoherent and speechless if we press evangelism upon him as a duty. It is a word that frightens him, partly because he thinks of it in the old pietistic terms and partly because it makes him conscious of a serious lack in his faith. We cannot expect him to have something of which he has never rightly heard.

The speechlessness is not a temporary accident but belongs as truly to the nature of the religion of which it is a manifestation as evangelism belongs to the nature of the Spirit-centered life of the early Christian. It is symptomatic of an individualistic religion in which each person takes care of his own relation with God. It is symptomatic of a moralistic religion in which the emphasis is upon character rather than upon grace. It is symptomatic of a strongly traditional religion in which conformity to the tradition is much more important than understanding; to think too much is to be tempted to be disloyal to the tradition. Individualistic, moralistic, traditional, are adjectives that describe the religion in which most of us have grown up. Let a man take seriously the importance of his own relation with God, let him live a good life, let him be loyal to the religious tradition of his denomination, and even his minister will be doubtful whether it is reasonable to expect anything more. He is a " good Christian." A minister whose church was comfortably full on Sunday mornings but whose congregation was almost totally unaware of the non-Christian world at its door was asked why his preaching consisted so largely of suggestions for moral improvement and had in it so little of a gospel of judgment and mercy. His answer was that he would be embarrassed to preach such a gospel to such good Christians as constituted his congregation. He could assume that they had heard the gospel and were Christians who needed only improvement. Not they but the people outside were the ones who needed to be called to repentance.

It is this myth of the "good Christian" which needs to be exploded. Jesus was highly critical of this use of the word "good" by the rich young ruler. "*Good* Master, what *good* thing must I do?" We have to distinguish then between what we mean by "good Christians" and what Jesus Christ expected of anyone who dared to follow him, between a church that is a society of religiously and morally superior people who are interested in their own improvement and a church of sinners who are being redeemed by the grace and mercy of God that they have come to know in Jesus Christ and who cannot rest satisfied as long as there is anyone who does not possess the secret of life that has been revealed to them. There is a basic falsity in the pose of the "good Christian"; there must always be a tension and anxiety beneath the surface of his mind lest the truth should be known that he is a sinner and he should lose his standing as a "good Christian." That in itself is sufficient to make a man speechless, for fear he may betray his inner inadequacy, uncertainty — and even his unbelief! But when we depend wholly upon the kindness of God to sinners and can pose as nothing other than unbelievers who are being redeemed by grace, it would be idiotic to conceal that there is both sin and unbelief in us. To the end of our days we have to confess our sin and unbelief, which are just two sides of the resistance of the world in us to God. We are no longer afraid to be honest either before God or before our fellow men, so that our tongues are unloosed. We do not have to be some special, perfect kind of Christian who never says anything wrong before we dare speak of what are actually the central and most important realities of our existence. It is sufficient that God has come to us in Jesus Christ, that he has liberated us from ourselves into the glorious life of the children of God, that he is no longer distant from us but is with us in each moment through the gift of his Spirit, and that he has bound us together within the fellowship of all who belong to him in all ages. He who is the truth has freed us not only from the bondage of sin but also from the bondage of spiritual unreality, incoherence, and speechlessness.

The honest recognition of our sin and unbelief provides also the bond between us and the world of sin and unbelief that is in need of evangelization. It is not a world apart from us that we approach from the outside; it is a world that we know from within ourselves. The unbeliever is therefore not a strange and alien creature who shocks us and whose attitude we cannot understand; rather, we recognize in him what we ourselves would be if it were not for what has met us in the Christian gospel. We understand him because we have been set free by God's acceptance of us to recognize all the thoughts and impulses and attitudes latent in our humanity that still form a resistance to God.

No Simple, Quick Solution

The recovery by the church and ministry of its evangelizing power is thus a much more complex problem than appears in most analyses and proposals. Short-range plans are likely after a time to create a false confidence that the problem has been reasonably well solved. The situation, rightly seen, shakes us as a church to the very roots of our being and challenges the validity of what passes as Christianity among us. The problem is nothing less than how the church of our day is to recover the power to be the church founded by Jesus Christ and perfectly incarnated in him. There are no quick remedies for the sickness from which we suffer. A church does not change its character overnight. But a church *can* change its character, not of itself but under the transforming influence of God's Word and Spirit. The trouble with us is that we expect to be able to accomplish almost any change by one or two nationwide six-week courses of training.

All aspects of the ministry discussed in this book are relevant to the recovery of evangelizing power. We cannot even know that we are something other than the church we are intended to be until the Scriptures are open in our hands and hearts, revealing to us God's intention. Only the preaching and teaching of God's word as it sounds from Scripture, faithfully persisted in for years, can transform the church from a religious and moral society into a fellowship of disciples with a clear consciousness of mission. There must also be an educational program that gives Christians the opportunity not only of finding their way into Scripture for themselves but also of clarifying the meaning of their faith and growing in the kind of understanding, both of their faith and of their fellow men, that equips them to be effective witnesses. The pastoral ministry when it is expanded by the enlistment and training of men and women to minister to their fellow men can become the very spearhead of the church's evangelism. But never dare it be forgotten that it cannot be left to any group, since every Christian is constantly having thrust upon him unique and unrepeatable opportunities for simple Christian witness, and he should be ready to take advantage of his opportunities when they come.

Perhaps a final note is needed about the word " witness." It is often taken to mean exclusively " saying something about Jesus Christ in order to convert another person." It may in some instances mean just that. But that is far too narrow a definition of " witness." Our witness consists of the words we speak and the actions we perform in relation to another person in which we take that person seriously as one who belongs together with us in the family of God; it may consist also of the patient silence in which we refrain from speaking and try to understand the person with whom we have to do. When we speak, the words will not necessarily be recognizably religious words. To talk religiously can in some intances be the surest way of alienating the person. There are no formulas for such words of witness. Perhaps our surest guidance is in the words of Jesus instructing the disciples what to do when they were brought before the courts of unbelievers. " In that hour it shall be given you what you are to say." If the mind and heart within us are nourished upon the gospel and we are unconditionally open toward God, we need only be concerned in our confrontation with any person to have an honest conversation in which our words correspond with reality. But let us be sure that we do not through timidity fail to say what God really gives us to say!

8

THE REBIRTH OF THE CHURCH

LOOKING back over the preceding chapters, one may have two contradictory impressions, the one that the ministry has been made to appear entirely too difficult, the other that it is all too simple. There is a danger that, in drawing out the picture of a ministry that is prophetic, priestly, kingly, Christlike, and apostolic, we may succeed only in sketching an impossible ideal that will drive even the most earnest pastor to despair. In so far as we have been guilty of that offense, the need now is to make plain what a simple thing it is in the last resort to find one's true ministry. God does not expect perfection of us in the ministry. He knows how human we are, how subject to intolerable pressures, how weak, how easily deluded and tempted to subtle forms of unfaithfulness. All he asks of us is that when he calls us we should answer and when he sends us we should go. The simplicity of our ministry is that it consists in letting ourselves be unconditionally at God's disposal. That is a large part of what is contained in the Old Testament term " servant " of God, which we translate " minister." " Slave of God " is actually what it means, thereby emphasizing the unconditional character of the believer's relationship with his Lord. The one question we have continually to ask ourselves is whether we are unconditionally at God's disposal. If we are, then the prophets and apostles will be our most congenial companions. We will find ourselves taken into the fellowship of our Lord himself as a friend rather than as a slave. And in such company God will surely equip us in some measure for a truly Biblical ministry.

The second and much greater danger is that we have made the problem of recovering the Biblical character of the ministry far too simple. The fact is easily recognized that in a large measure the ministry has lost its Biblical character and has been shaped into modern forms that are essentially alien to the Biblical tradition. Expository preaching has disappeared. The prophetic voice has been replaced by a softer and more soothing voice. The church has been taken out of the service of God's disturbing gospel and has been humanized as an institution to provide men and women with the spiritual comfort and security they need. This is very bad. But fortunately, now that we have recognized what is wrong, we can do something about it. We must get back at once to sound Biblical exposition. We must recapture the prophetic note in our preaching. We must reshape our ministries according to the pattern that is provided for us by the apostles. It is all so simple. But is it?

We may begin by examining more carefully the word " Biblical," which has been used frequently in speaking of the Biblical character of the ministry. We have assumed that anyone who is observant can see what is Biblical. We have proceeded blithely on the assumption that the Scriptures are somehow a unity in what they have to say concerning the ministry, when actually the assertion of any real unity in the Scriptures is hotly contested in the field of Biblical scholarship and the restatement of it is one of our most difficult problems in Biblical research. It is not many years since the consensus of the scholars was in the direction of finding only a variety of religions or theologies in both the Old and the New Testaments. The religion of Jesus and the religion of Paul were sharply distinguished from each other. The process of Israel's evolution was traced stage by stage from a primitive animistic religion to the lofty heights of ethical monotheism in the eighth-century prophets, which then declined into the more static forms of Judaism. A certain thread of unity might be traced historically from one religion of the Bible to the other, but each was recognized as different in nature, so that any attempt to formulate a Biblical faith or a Biblical theology or a Biblical ministry was considered to be contrary to the well-documented facts. More recently the trend in scholarship has been toward the recognition of unity in the midst of this diversity. Jesus and Paul are no longer set in such sharp antithesis to each other, and a very definite unity is claimed for the New Testament as a whole. In Switzerland, Germany, France, and Holland, a very considerable number of books on Old Testament theology have appeared in the last twenty-five years, each in its own way tracing a unity in the midst of the diverse religious phenomena of the Old Testament. More recently theologies of the New Testament have begun to appear. But the subject that has been approached with most timidity is that of the unity of the Bible as a whole. The fear of Biblical scholars has been lest a false unity should be superimposed upon the Bible that would conceal the diverse historical realities that have been brought to light by two hundred years of careful scholarly research. But the problem can no longer be ignored, and the discussions now under way concerning the unity of the Bible are likely to be of great and fruitful significance for the life of the church. What must be emphasized, however, is that a vast amount of work needs to be done in the field of Biblical and theological research before we can speak with confidence of a " Biblical " character of anything, and that we have to use such language with restraint, recognizing that the question what is to be taken as normative in the Scriptures as a whole is wide open to debate. The problem of a Biblical ministry is inseparable, therefore, from the problem of a Biblical theology.

This interrelation of ministry and theology, the recognition that the character of the ministry is determined by the character of the theology that underlies it, exposes another aspect of the complexity of our problem. We cannot expect any essential change in the character of the ministry unless there is a change in the theology of ministers. If we have lost continuity with the Biblical line of ministry, it is because we have lost continuity with the Biblical line of thinking and being. Always beneath the pattern of our conduct lies a pattern of thought and conviction and some basic resolution of the nature of our being in relation to God. The systematic elucidation of these substructures of our life takes place in some theology or other. There is a real sense in which we never rightly know who we are until we find a theology that is for us the ultimate expression of truth (at least for the time being). That theology is an objectification of the inner reality of our existence. Confusion in theology is certain, therefore, to issue in a confused ministry, and there is no likelihood of recovering a prophetic or apostolic ministry unless our thinking begins to approximate in some way the thinking of the prophets and the apostles.

We appreciate the difficulty of our situation, then, only when we take full account of the unbiblical nature of the theologies that are most widely current in our churches. The most significant development in our seminaries in recent years is the rebirth of interest in Biblical theology, but if we are honest, we must acknowledge that it has not penetrated very far into the life of the churches. They are still largely under the spell of theologies that had their origin in the nineteenth century. What follows is only a rough sketch of the situation drawn with broad strokes. There is a pietism that interprets the word "spiritual" as the direct opposite to material and encourages men in thinking that the concern of the church must be only with the souls of men and not with the wider and more concrete situations that confront them in daily life, an individualism and a spirituality that are essentially alien to the Bible. There is a religious humanism that knows no other god than the divine potentiality in man, that incorporates into itself every movement for the betterment of man's lot, claiming the name "Christian" because of Jesus' supreme compassion for man and yet forced to discard almost the entire theological framework of the Bible as an outworn mythology. There is a superficial moralism that probes no question deeply but values the Christian religion highly as a means of keeping personal and social life steady and secure: religion as the bulwark of Western civilization, the church as the guardian of the American way of life, Christian education as a safeguard for our children to keep them from becoming delinquents. There is a Biblicism that uses the Bible as a means of fastening upon the minds of men social prejudices, barren religious formulas, and rigidly legalistic codes of conduct that a Jeremiah or a Jesus or a Paul would break through as forms of spiritual slavery. But these are most likely theologies that most of us can easily see through and reject, so that we are not touched by the problem in ourselves. We have not spoken the truth until we own that in spite of our earnestness about Christian truth we who are ministers have had to acknowledge to ourselves again and again that we have been the dupes of error. What has been our experience across the years with this Bible in which God confronts us with his truth and through which he sends to us his Spirit? If we have let it speak its own word freely instead of forcing our cocksure interpretations upon it, has it not more than once torn down our neat theological structures and left us in dismay to begin all over again our task of theological understanding and theological construction? The Bible is by its nature the enemy of all our false theologies, and it has a work of destruction to do in our churches in order to clear the way for a more truly Biblical theology that would then be the basis for a more truly Biblical ministry. Can we in honesty say that the battle has really begun in the American church?

The Interrelation of Church and Ministry

A third complication in our problem arises from the interrelation of church and ministry. The ministry does not stand alone and cannot be considered in isolation. Minister and church are mutually dependent and mutually responsible to each other for what they are. The ministry reflects the strengths and weaknesses of the church out of which it comes, and if no way is found to break the vicious circle, it proceeds to accentuate and consolidate those same strengths and weaknesses. It is unfair to castigate a minister for superficial moralism who has known nothing else for the first eighteen years of his life and whose congregation smiles on him only when he gives them bright, popular fifteen-minute talks on how to be happy and good. But it is equally unfair to be harsh toward a congregation that refuses to hear anything about its Christian responsibility in economics and politics if it has never been shown from the Scriptures that the God and Father of Jesus Christ is deeply concerned with what happens to his family in the whole of its existence. There is no defect in the Christian ministry for which there is not a corresponding defect in the life of the church. If we have an unbiblical ministry, we have also an unbiblical church, a church that fails to stand in direct line with the church that we see in the Scriptures. The two problems must be faced together because they are two aspects of a single problem.

This interrelation of church and ministry needs to be taken with the greatest seriousness if we are to make any headway in the solution of the complex problems of the ministry. The idea is widespread that all that it takes to make a strong church is an able minister. So if things do not go well, the thing to do is to change the minister. It does not occur to anyone that what may be needed is a radical change in the character of the congregation. The word that sounds from the pulpit has little or nothing of its evangelical power until it becomes enfleshed, incarnated, in the persons who constitute the congregation. Not until in them it is a word that is acted out in the common daily life of the community is it translated into terms that are comprehensible and convincing to the man or woman who needs to be persuaded. All our talk about God's love is an empty mouthing of words unless that strange and incomprehensible love of God, which was actuality in Jesus Christ, becomes actuality in us in our relations with those with whom we have to do day by day. We as preachers are engaged in a work of translation as we preach; we are translating the words of Scripture out of their ancient setting into the language of our contemporary world. But our verbal translation is insufficient. Our words must become flesh in us who preach, and then they must become flesh in those who hear; they must be lived out joyfully or painfully, syllable by syllable, until the life of the Christian fellowship becomes in itself a proclamation of the gospel and a convincing witness to the truth of the gospel. How can its truth be believed until there is a body of people who are willing to stake their lives upon its truth? It is surely obvious that nothing is more productive of unbelief than glaring contradictions between the doctrines proclaimed from the pulpit and the doctrines by which the members of the congregation actually guide their daily lives. We must get the idea firmly wedged into the minds of our people that it is not the preacher who has the most difficult task in the proclamation of the gospel. He bears the word only the first stage of the way. If it is to reach its destination, they must take it from him and carry it to its destination in a world that is in critical need of a word from God; and that is the more difficult task.

It becomes clear, then, that what we are aiming at and what we are hoping for is nothing less than a rebirth of the church. It is not just the ministry but the church as a whole that has need to recover its Biblical character. The problem of the ministry cannot be solved apart from the problem of the church. We shall do well in our theological seminaries to recognize this larger context of our problem because at times we think and speak as though the character of the ministry were our special problem quite apart from the problem of the character of the church, and as though we and we alone can solve the problem by reformulating our conception of the ministry and revising our theological curriculum that it may produce the desired article. Certainly the theological seminary has a major responsibility in this matter, and careful studies of what is being made of the ministry in our time and of what might be made of it if we understood better what we are doing and why, are of great value and significance, especially when they are carried out with the thoroughness that is evident in the recent work of Drs. Niebuhr and Williams. But there is no formula or program for the reshaping of the ministry that is proof against the pressures that are at work constantly in the life of the church molding a ministry that will conform to the desires of the existent church. Dr. Niebuhr has sketched for us a noble ideal of the ministry in his " pastoral director " who, as the chief minister of the church, co-ordinates and guides the ministries of a host of others who share his tasks with him. But all of us know pressures from within ourselves, from within the organizations of our churches, and from the administration-minded society in which we live that can subtly and very quickly transform the pastoral director into an executive director. A pastoral director is possible only in a church where a considerable number of members are committed to sharing in the ministries of the church and are willing to submit themselves to the kind of training and spiritual disciplines that will equip them for those ministries. That in turn is the product of a different understanding of the gospel and a different conception of what it means to be a Christian than is common in most of our churches.

The Deceptiveness of Appearances

It has always been difficult to know when the church is most in need of renewal. In the middle of the eighth century b.c. in Israel, religious institutions seemed to the outward eye to be in a flourishing condition. The sanctuaries at Bethel and elsewhere were crowded with worshipers. It was a prosperous time and the Israelites were prepared not only to give their God the credit for their prosperity but also to contribute generously to the support of religion. Yet the prophet Amos declared at Bethel that the nation was hovering on the brink of an abyss, the beauty of its religious festivals being only a deceptive surface covering that hid the festering sores of this people's actual existence. Amos judged the spiritual health of the nation not by the success of its religious institutions but by the quality of life that he found in the homes, in the market place, in the relations of employers and workmen, in the councils of government, and in the law courts. He took Israel's spiritual pulse not when they were enraptured by the music and drama of religious ritual but when they were living their normal, everyday life. And he pronounced people, priests, and prophets in need of a drastic new beginning if they were ever to be useful to God in the fulfillment of his purpose for the world.

Or we might look at the Christian church of Europe in the year
A.D. 1500. To the outward eye it was a most impressive institution.
The whole of Europe was dotted with its massive cathedrals and
its parish churches, and the whole of European society and culture
was unified under its direction. Kings trembled before the authority of the church, and businessmen did not dare to disobey its
commands. There were evils in both church and society and
weaknesses in the ministry of the church, but what were they in
comparison with the glory and magnificence of the church as it
held the whole world in its control? It is no wonder that some
historians go into rhapsodies as they depict the medieval church
and medieval society and condemn the Reformers soundly for
their rude disruption of such a marvelously stable order of life.
And yet the Reformers were not wrong when they declared the
church and ministry of their day to be in need of a thorough renewal. The church for all its impressiveness was a hollow structure and its clergy were hollow men. If the Reformers had not
sought to change it from within, there would have been other
forces in a rapidly changing world that would have shattered it
from without.

So also today the church in our land is an impressive institution. The world has never seen its like. Sixty-two per cent of the
citizens of our communities are members of some religious organization. Our churches are full on Sundays. Hundreds of millions
of dollars are spent on new churches. Our annual budgets for
work at home and abroad are of staggering dimensions. There
are individual congregations that spend half a million dollars a
year. We blanket the world with our missionaries. Moreover, the
church occupies a very influential position in American society.
No man in a public position would dare to speak disrespectfully
of it or of its faith. Even the agnostic and the atheist speak softly
for fear of rousing its wrath against them. The church in America is in a very strong position, and this fact makes it fearfully
hard for anyone to believe that the church is in peril of its life
or that the church is in radical need of an inner reformation. Yet
Amos, if he were alive today, would not have to make any serious
alterations in his sermons before he spoke them as his message

from God to our American situation. And Luther would be aghast at what we have made of the church that had its rebirth in the Reformation.

The strength of the church never resides in its numbers or in its wealth or in its outward impressiveness. Its strength is to be measured from within and is determined by the extent to which it is true to its nature as the body of Jesus Christ, as the servant of the Word of God, as the human instrument through which he sets forward his redemptive purpose in the midst of the world. Let the church be what its Lord intended it to be and it is impregnable; no power on earth and no power out of the pit of hell can destroy it. But let the church be untrue to its calling and destiny, let it give itself in any measure into the service of any other Lord or any other gospel, and by that internal failure it has laid itself open to destruction. The true defense of the church, therefore, is not to declare war on a multitude of enemies that seem to threaten it from without — communism and materialism and humanism and agnosticism and atheism — but to acknowledge that the only enemy that can defeat us is already within our gates and within our hearts and minds, and has to be fought with weapons other than we use against external aggressors.

A Biblically-minded church is a church that understands from its reading of the Scriptures and from its study of its own history in the light of Scripture that as a human church it is constantly exposed to forces that deflect it from its purpose and tempt it to become unfaithful to its nature. The story of Israel in the Old Testament is the story of a people that came into being in response to God's call for a nation that would serve him, but that found it desperately difficult in each succeeding age to remain faithful to that call. They were constantly tempted to turn their special destiny from God into a special position of privilege with God and to make it the basis of a stultifying self-righteousness. And first among the peoples of Palestine and then among the nations where they lived in exile they were under pressure to conform to the patterns of life about them and to renounce the distinctiveness of a life in covenant with a God of righteousness and truth. A true Israel was preserved only by God's gift to them of a succession of prophets who warned them of their internal danger and called them to a renewal of their covenant with God.

Also in the New Testament the church confesses that the most serious dangers to its existence come not from without but from within. Judas, who betrayed his Lord, was a disciple. The book of The Acts pictures no ideal flawless church; it pictures a vital church, a church alive with power because it is so completely indwelt by its Lord, but also a church that would never have laid hold on its world mission if it had not been for new revelations that were granted to Peter and to Paul. From Paul's letters we learn the full story of how powerful an element there was in the earliest church that resisted bitterly a doctrine of justification by faith alone and hated Paul for opening the door so widely to the Gentile world. Even the Christian church of the first half century needed repentance and rebirth if it was to be kept from falsifying its nature and missing its destiny.

THE PROTESTANT AND THE ROMAN CONCEPTIONS OF THE CHURCH

It is this Biblical insight into the constant imperilment of the church from within which is missing in the Roman understanding of the church but which is the distinctive mark of the Protestant mind when it is truly Protestant. The Roman Church says, "We are the church of Jesus Christ, the one authoritative continuation in the world of the presence and power of Jesus Christ himself." The Protestant Church with equal boldness says, "We are the church of Jesus Christ, through which he continues today his redemptive work," but at once it goes on in a humbler vein and confesses: "We have failed again and again to be the church that God calls us to be. We have been unfaithful servants of God's Word, and our only hope is that he will grant us true repentance and renewal through the power of his Word and Spirit." In short, as Protestants we must acknowledge that we can remain the church that we claim to be only through a process of repeated reformations. A Reformed church thus is not a church that was reformed once and for all four hundred years ago, but rather it is a church that is continually being reformed as it comes under the judgment and hears anew the promise of God's word in Scripture. Here, then, is the essential difference between Romanism and Protestantism. Romanism identifies the empirical church, with its doctrines and practices and hierarchical order, with the divine-human reality of the body of Christ. Nowhere does that come more clearly to expression than in its claim of infallibility for the pope. His voice when he speaks ex cathedra is the voice of God without possibility of human error. A human person is identified unambiguously with God. Protestantism sees in that a falsification of the church of the Scriptures. The church dare not go to the opposite extreme, as it has sometimes done, and assume some more modest task than that of being God's representative and spokesman on earth. It has to claim equally with Romanism that in it resides the very presence and power and authority of Jesus Christ himself. The awful responsibility of its ministry is that it undertakes to speak words in which God himself will speak to men and to perform acts in which men will know the healing, life-transforming touch of Jesus Christ. But never dare we identify our human, empirical church unambiguously with the body of Jesus Christ or our ministry with the ministry of Jesus Christ. We have to say at one and the same time that by God's grace we are the church and that by our human weakness and sinfulness we are not the church. And in that seemingly contradictory confession lies the dynamic of Protestantism. Remove the negative confession, and the church, however successful it may be outwardly, becomes static in its essential existence.

Sometimes Protestant churches are tempted to ape the Roman assurance. They are so confident that their doctrines and practices are completely Christian that they see no need for repentance or reformation within themselves. Their assurance of identity with the one and only truly Biblical and apostolic church may become so great that they assert an exclusive claim for themselves and, like the Roman Church, set a question mark against all forms of Christianity existing outside their own borders. What they fail to see is that in ceasing to set a question mark against their own form of Christianity and their own church, they have by that failure lost for themselves the essential mark of a Biblical church, that it is always a church that knows that judgment begins at the house of God.

W. A. Visser 't Hooft, in the introduction to his *The Renewal of the Church* (The Westminster Press, 1957), states very clearly the Protestant position. We acknowledge in faith the existence within the church of a true body of Christ into which we have been received and by which we are sustained in the Christian life. This body of Christ need not and cannot be renewed. But we have also to acknowledge our responsibility within an empirical, historical church that at many points stands in contradiction to the body of Christ and is constantly in need of renewal. The church is both a divine reality and a human reality, and we err when we ignore either aspect. There has been a church through the centuries in spite of all the blindness and unfaithfulness of men because God needs a church to serve his redemptive purpose and God has ever preserved for himself a faithful witness but never has God permitted his human witnesses to have their security in themselves. He has left them exposed to human weaknesses and errors for two very good reasons: first, that only in that exposed condition are they open toward the world of humanity and so a channel of communication for God's grace and truth to man, and secondly, that only a church that finds no point of absolute security in itself will be completely open toward God and willing to put itself unconditionally in his hands.

THE PROSPECT FOR THE FUTURE

Perhaps now we may be permitted to ask the question, Are there signs of renewal in the life of the Protestant church today? To this we must return a somewhat hesitant answer, confident and hopeful and yet chastened, recognizing that a rebirth of the church may have an abortive outcome through the wrong kind of confidence. It is possible without being untruthful to draw a picture of the church and its ministry today that is very black and has in it few signs of any promise. It is very easy to become cynical about the church, and this is often a serious problem for students in the years of training before they have to assume concrete responsibility for its ministry. (The problem then is of their going to the opposite extreme and becoming uncritical.) But there are also signs of hope, signs that God is at work in our midst reshaping for himself a church that will be more amenable to his redemptive purpose. In summarizing these signs we may in some measure retrace some portions of ground that we have already covered.

The first such sign is the reopening of the Scriptures. Within the past thirty years Biblical scholarship has been revolutionized by the combination of thorough historical and literary research with a new theological grasp of the meaning of revelation.

But it would be folly to suggest that more than the first steps have been taken toward theological renewal in Biblical studies. Many questions of paramount importance have hardly even been discussed as yet. In America there is still a very strong resistance among Biblical scholars against even the recognition of their theological responsibility. Many fear that unless Biblical scholarship confines itself to philological, archaeological, historical, and literary questions, it will lose its scientific character. It does not occur to them that, since the character of a science must be determined by its object, Biblical scholarship can be a science adequate to the nature of its object, the Bible, only when it is able to take full account of its theological content. In Britain and on the Continent there seems to be a tendency in some quarters for the theological renewal to follow an erratic course. A failure to think through the problem of the unity of the Testaments in twentieth-century terms is causing the reassertion of the centrality of Jesus Christ to the whole Bible to issue in a reversion to allegorical and typological interpretations of the Old Testament, a development that could have tragic consequences. One should perhaps mention also the growing influence of Bultmann, who denies that the Old Testament is Christian Scripture and who by his process of demythologizing manages to eliminate also from the New Testament almost all the theological elements that are summarized in the Apostles' Creed. Our hope is thus of necessity a chastened hope with full consciousness of the vast labors in critical scholarship that the church requires if the hope is to be fulfilled.

The second sign of hope is the rebirth of a critical theology in the church. During the nineteenth century the theological issues became defined in such a way that theology was much more at home in the university than in the church. It became more academic than churchly, more centered in the questions of the scholar than in the questions of the believer. Two illustrations should be sufficient. One is found in the shift of interest at the end of the nineteenth century from the study of doctrine to the study of religion. Forty years ago systematic theology seemed to be on the way out. There was little concern in the church about the formulation of Christian beliefs. There was even a widespread impression that the abandonment of doctrinal concern in the church was a liberation for the spirit of man. No longer would antiquated doctrines hold him back from the recognition of truth in all its breadth and richness. The interest was not in doctrine but in religious phenomena and religions, Christian and non-Christian, and there was an expectation that out of the scientific investigation of all the religious manifestations of the human race there would emerge a final, objective definition of religion that would point the way for us into the future. Philosophy of religion was a necessity in order to interpret the diverse phenomena and to explore the relationship between the truth of religion and truth as it was being manifested in all other realms of human research. But somehow in more recent years as the graduate in theology moved out of the academic world into the church he found it increasingly difficult to maintain his interest in the philosophy of religion. It neither asked nor answered the questions that were matters of life or death for him as the minister of a parish. He could do without it. What he needed more than anything else was some clear guidance concerning the nature of the faith to which he and the church were committed by their relationship to

Jesus Christ; and a theology that failed to give him that guidance failed to maintain his interest. So it is that the past quarter century has seen a rebirth of interest in doctrine. Christians confronted with aggressive non-Christian faiths have found vague formulations of religion innocuous and have demanded to know with definiteness what the Christian faith has to say concerning God and man and the meaning of life.

In so far as this renewed doctrinal interest results only in a new orthodoxy, it ceases to be a sign of hope. Nothing is more deadly than the taking over of a seemingly more tenable doctrinal formula as a substitute for genuine theological thinking. What we need in the church is not, as someone has said, "an intellectually tenable formulation of evangelical doctrine," but rather an awakening of the church at large, and of the ministry in particular, to its ongoing theological responsibility. Theology is the discipline by means of which the church is able to do something about its dilemma between truth and error. We are constantly in that dilemma because we are a human, sinful church living in a human, sinful world. Both in our doctrine and in our being we are each day guilty of falsifying the gospel. Each time we preach we know that there has been a measure of falsehood mingled with our truth and that our falsehood is the enemy of our gospel. Only a critical theology that brings the life and doctrine of the church under the criterion of God's revelation of the true church in his word in Scripture can help us in this situation and deliver us out of our paralyzing errors into the freedom of the truth. What greater sign of hope could there be for us than that a theology that so understands itself should begin to show itself here and there in the church?

A third sign of hope is the increasingly widespread concern about the unity of the church, particularly as it has come to expression in the ecumenical movement. We must distinguish between two different kinds of concern about unity that ought not to be confused with each other. There is one form of it that might be called an indiscriminate passion for unification. It condemns all denominational separateness as evil, attributes most of

the weaknesses of the church to that separateness, and hopes by
a process of external unification to create one great powerful
church for the future. Enthusiasts for that kind of unification are
usually impatient of doctrinal discussions, assuming without discussion that we are already one on most essential points and that
the chief obstacles to unification are merely a few points in church
order. The second form has little in common with the first. It
begins with the fact that we are all one in so far as we are members of the body of Jesus Christ, that oneness is not primarily
a future possibility to be achieved by our efforts but rather is
God's gift to us in Jesus Christ. In him, God has made us one in
spite of all the things that divide us. It is impossible for there to
be more than one people of God, one body of Jesus Christ. To
insist upon separation from any true believer who acknowledges
Jesus Christ as his Lord and who receives the Holy Spirit as the
living center of his existence is to separate ourselves from Jesus
Christ himself and to reject the fellowship of the Holy Spirit. In
the strength of this oneness we are able then to face with openness
and honesty the problems that arise from our dividedness. We are
able to hold conversations about our differences in the spirit of
both truth and charity. We cease to demand unity peremptorily,
because in faith we possess a measure of unity that gives us hope
of a yet greater oneness that we may have with one another in
Christ in years to come. It is significant that this second approach
to unity has had greater prominence than the other in the thinking of the World Council of Churches.

A fourth sign of hope may be seen in the awakening concern
of the church about evangelism. The preceding chapter has
shown that here also our hope is a chastened hope. We thank God
for the new openness of the churches to the reality of the problem,
but we have seen reason to doubt whether the full depth of the
problem has yet begun to be grasped. Perhaps the greatest reason
for hope is something that is usually an occasion of despair, the
uncovering of the face of unbelief in one region of the world after
another to stand bold and unashamed before the church as a
world that is antithetical to the church. God apparently has no

way of making us take him seriously as the God that he is except by unveiling to us a world that says " No " to the church and its gospel. Whether or not it is also a " No " to him we must hesitate to say.

There is yet another sign of hope, one that may prove highly significant: the rising interest and concern of laymen to understand their ministry and to receive training that they may discharge it more adequately. In many parts of the church across the world, centers are springing up where laymen gather for periods, brief or more extended, to study and discuss together how best they may serve the church. Hendrik Kraemer's invaluable book *A Theology of the Laity* (The Westminster Press, 1958) provides not only a survey of the part that laymen have played in the life of the church from the time of the apostles to the present day and of the international character of the movement in recent years but also an indication of how slow the churches have been to recognize the undeveloped resources for ministry that they possess in their laymen.

There has long been an unfortunate misconception abroad in the church that the encouragement of laymen to consider themselves ministers of Christ is likely to bring in its train a lowering of standards and a depreciation of the importance of the ordained ministry. " When every man thinks himself a minister, what place will remain for a special ministry? " This apprehension has a valid ground in the widespread conception of the priesthood of all believers as constituting every Christian his own priest or minister. Many a Protestant takes for granted that that doctrine of the Reformation is in its essence a repudiation of all need for a special priesthood, since every Christian, having direct access to God, can be his own priest and needs, at least in principle, no one to minister to him. This results in Christians taking a falsely individualistic attitude in their faith that is destructive of the Christian community and logically would make the church itself unnecessary. Also, perhaps more often than we realize, it leads them to think they should be able to minister to their own spiritual needs when they desperately need someone to minister to them in the name of Christ. The priesthood of all believers, every Christian a minister, when understood out of the Scriptures means that every Christian should be a minister to his fellow men and decidedly not that every Christian is his own minister. No man can be his own minister. No matter how highly he may be trained for the ministry and no matter how disciplined he is in his spiritual life, he needs someone to minister to him in the name of Jesus Christ, to speak to him a word that is a word from God to him, to intercede for him before the throne of God, to confront him as Christ's ambassador. When we become ministers we need not less but more that someone should perform this ministry toward us, and we should be all the more capable of benefiting from it. This is the chief justification for the episcopal office, that it should provide this all-important ministry to ministers and not become a mere administrative office. And there is need in nonepiscopal churches to make provision for such a ministry. Why, then, should we think that when laymen know themselves called to a ministry, this will lessen the need for a special ministry? The opposite should be true: that the more conscious the laity are of their own priesthood, the more ready they will be to profit from the ministrations of those who are farther on than themselves in the understanding and exercise of Christ's ministry.

All lay movements in the church are not equally hopeful. Some have been conceived merely as agencies to enlist a more vigorous support for the existing institution and to provide an additional channel for the promotion of church programs. Some have tended, at least in their national conferences, to have more the atmosphere of a meeting of the National Association of Manufacturers than of a seriously Christian enterprise. But these are mere froth on the surface of a much deeper movement. It is seen at its best in such centers as Kerk en Wereld in Holland, Männerdorf in Switzerland, the evangelical academies in Germany, the Iona Community in Scotland, Sigtuna in Sweden, the Ecumenical Institute in Switzerland, and similar organizations patterned on these that are coming into being in Canada, United

States, Japan, and other parts of the world. Leadership is being given by the Department on the Laity of the World Council of Churches. On this deeper level the problems on which study focuses are those in which the layman sees his own distinctive ministry, standing as he does in the painful gap between the church and the world. This is hopeful, but it will become even more hopeful when the movement begins to affect the pattern of lay life in the local Christian congregation.

We are called to be the church of Jesus Christ. We are called to be ministers of Jesus Christ. In him alone we see the church and the ministry fulfilled. In him alone can it be said that the church is what it was intended to be. In his ministry alone is there no disobedience or unfaithfulness. But where the church and the ministry are complete there stands a cross, and it is into the church and ministry of a crucified Christ that we dare to enter — crucified, yet also risen. There is no entrance for us into our true ministry unless we die with him and rise with him into that newness of life which in his risen power he shares with those who are bonded together in fellowship with him. And the reward of our ministry is just this — that he should count us worthy to be taken into fellowship with him and to be members of his body.

REFERENCES

The following list contains the books from which quotations have been taken or to which reference has been made.

Davies, W. D., *Paul and Rabbinic Judaism*. The Macmillan Company, 1950.

Dodd, C. H., *According to the Scriptures*. Charles Scribner's Sons, 1953.

Elliott, Harrison, *Can Religious Education Be Christian?* The Macmillan Company, 1940.

Herberg, Will, *Protestant-Catholic-Jew*. Doubleday & Co., Inc., 1955.

Hiltner, Seward, *Preface to Pastoral Theology*. Abingdon Press, 1958.

Jenkins, Daniel T., *The Gift of Ministry*. Faber & Faber, Ltd., London, 1947.

Johnson, A. R., *The Cultic Prophet in Ancient Israel*. University of Wales Press, Cardiff, 1944.

Koestler, Arthur, *Darkness at Noon*. The Macmillan Company, 1948.

Kraemer, Hendrik, *A Theology of the Laity*. The Westminster Press, 1958.

Morgan, Charles, *Liberties of the Mind*. The Macmillan Company, 1951.

Niebuhr, H. Richard, *The Purpose of the Church and Its Ministry*. Harper & Brothers, 1956.

Niebuhr, H. Richard and Williams, Daniel D., *The Ministry in Historical Perspectives*. Harper & Brothers, 1956.

Niebuhr, H. Richard, Williams, Daniel D., and Gustafson, James M., *The Advancement of Theological Education*. Harper & Brothers, 1957.

Nygren, Anders, *Christ and His Church*. The Westminster Press, 1956.

Parker, T. H. L., *The Oracles of God*. Lutterworth Press, 1947.

Pittenger, W. Norman, *The Church, the Ministry, and Reunion*. The Seabury Press, 1957.

Ramsey, A. M., *The Gospel and the Catholic Church*. Longmans, Green and Company, 1956.

Rowley, H. H., *The Biblical Doctrine of Election*. Lutterworth Press, 1950.

Smart, James D., *The Teaching Ministry of the Church*. The Westminster Press, 1954.

Tillich, Paul, *Systematic Theology*, Vol. I. University of Chicago Press, 1951.

Torrance, Thomas F., *Royal Priesthood*. Alec Allenson, 1955.

Visser 't Hooft, W. A., *The Renewal of the Church*. The Westminster Press, 1957.

Von Allmen, J. J., *Diener Sind Wir*. Quell Verlag, 1958.

Welch, Adam C., *Prophet and Priest in Old Israel*. S.C.M. Press, Ltd., London, 1936.

Welch, Claude, *The Reality of the Church*. Charles Scribner's Sons, 1958.

INDEX